Front Cover Image: Emma Lou Standing Water Hart. Author's Photo.

Back Cover Image: Cheyenne-Arapho Bead Workers. Photo 1900, no. 19383.90.1 Barde Collection. Courtesy, Research Division of the Oklahoma Historical Society.

NISH' KI:
Cheyenne Grandmothers

Pillars of Strength

KAY SCHWEINFURTH

authorHOUSE®

AuthorHouse™
1663 Liberty Drive, Suite 200
Bloomington, IN 47403
www.authorhouse.com
Phone: 1-800-839-8640

First published by AuthorHouse 5/13/2009

ISBN: 978-1-4389-2297-3 (sc)
ISBN: 978-1-4389-2298-0 (hc)

Library of Congress Control Number: 2008909644

Printed in the United States of America
Bloomington, Indiana

This book is printed on acid-free paper.

Table of Contents

Abbreviations in the Text

AFDC—Aid to Families with Dependent Children

BIA—Bureau of Indian Affairs

CAR—Cheyenne and Arapaho Report

COP—Census of the Population

CETA—Comprehensive Education and Training Act

CRH—Civil Rights Hearing

DO—Daily Oklahoman

ECDN—Elk City Daily News

HA—Hammon Advocate

*HHS—*Health and Human Services

IHS—Indian Health Trends and Services

LF—Loretta Fowler

MJW—Mary Jane Warde

NIYC—National Indian Youth Commission

OJ—Oklahoma Journal

RCIA—U.S. Congress Report Commission of Indian Affairs

SSI—Social Supplemental Income

USDA—U.S. Department of Agriculture

USDOC—U.S. Department of Commerce

WR—*Watonga Republican*

WOHP—Washita Oral History Project

Preface

In 1974 I began four years of recording oral histories and collecting primary documents from an Indian–white Oklahoma community. This was a requirement for a doctoral degree in social anthropology at the University of Oklahoma. I completed the required dissertation, and upon its approval, requested that some material be withheld from publication for ten years or longer. I never intended to permanently suppress the material, but two elderly Cheyenne women, who had been forthright about revealing their everyday stresses and relationships with other members of the Indian community, requested that material I had gathered not be published until sometime after their deaths. They were concerned about remarks they might have made to me during that period of time about their relatives and friends that could be open to unintended interpretation. One person, in particular, worried that her close friends might guess that she had made an unkind remark that would summon a vengeful ghost.

As these women revealed their lives of hardship to an outsider, they always spoke openly with insight and wit. But when speaking about each other, they were inclined to speak in hushed tones and with a tacit understanding of confidentiality. Occasionally a Cheyenne woman would express ambivalence about having her view of the community or the outside world recorded and published, because she believed that outsiders would somehow misconstrue the information. Yet several others thought the Cheyenne community needed some exposure concerning its problems and believed that it might help outsiders understand them better and treat them more fairly.

One of my most candid collaborators was Anna Hawk. I met Anna at the annual Linguistics Institute in Norman, Oklahoma, in the summer of 1974. She was one of a group of American Indians who was teaching Christian missionaries the basics of how to learn to speak and understand the unwritten language of an indigenous people. The missionaries needed to acquire this skill because they were going to developing countries where no one spoke English.

Anna, who was born at the turn of the century, was an accomplished speaker of the Cheyenne language, and she possessed a vast storehouse of tribal lore and history. She had a vivid memory for detail, and she was perceptive, quick-witted, and loved conversation. Up front she told me that she had not participated in the state of Oklahoma oral history project in the 1960s because she did not like the way it was being run and questioned its authenticity. "Besides," Anna said, "some of 'em just made up stories to make money." Of course that is a possible hazard in the recording of any oral history, but after spending a great deal of time with these families, it was possible for me to check different versions of stories with other family members. The procedure was by no means one hundred percent error proof, because it finally became a judgment call. When, however, someone could not remember an important detail, he or she would think about it for a while and remember, but sometimes not. Then someone else might recall the event or matter in great detail.

In the course of time Anna introduced me to her many friends and relatives, some of whom I came to know as well as I knew her. I spent a great deal of time with Anna before her death three years later in 1977. Shortly before she died, I promised her I would take responsibility for her teenage grandson, Junior, also called Freeman, which I did. Junior lived in my home for eight months while he attended an Oklahoma City Catholic high school and worked part time at a nearby fast food restaurant.

When Junior arrived at my home, the first thing he wanted to do was to look for a job so he could have some spending money. Although he was willing to make the effort, he was reticent. He was convinced that he could not be hired by anyone, "because" he said, "Indians do not get jobs." I assured him that he could, and that he surely must try. I went with him to look. He was offered a job at each of the three places that we went. A surprised but happy Junior took the job at the Roy Rogers restaurant, and he quickly made himself valuable by working harder than anyone else. He stayed after closings many times to make certain that everything was spotlessly clean. But one day he came home unexpectedly, because he had worn an Indian belt to work, and the cowboy restaurant manager told him to go home and change belts because, he said, "Indian get-ups do not belong in a cowboy restaurant." Junior had one other problem at the restaurant. No matter how hard he tried, he could not bring himself to greet each arriving customer with an enthusiastic, "Howdy."

He had great difficulty adjusting to his new environment at school also. The athletic coach urged the tall Indian boy with the athletic physique to sign up for one of the school sports, but Junior declined to participate, much to the other students' consternation. School was not easy for him. His English teacher reported that he had less self-confidence than any other student she had, so it was no surprise to me that after eight months he made the decision to go to his mother's home in North Dakota.

I was a newly widowed mother of three daughters when I began field trips to Hammon, a Cheyenne Indian–white community in western Oklahoma. Hammon is located only eighteen miles from my natal home, a lucky circumstance that helped considerably with the logistics of balancing schedules of three daughters with schedules of a relatively large Cheyenne community. The Hammon Cheyenne were reported to be hostile to outsiders, but making friends was relatively easy for me, in part because I was a single mother with children, as was almost every Cheyenne woman I met. All of us were women living alone with children to care for, and all of us had experienced the death of a loved one early in life. Although our environments were markedly different, many of our challenges were surprisingly similar.

My relationship with the white Hammon community was cordial. I had grown up in close proximity to this rural Indian–white community, and I knew most of the local farmers, all of whom were white. As a teenager I had worked on Saturdays and during the summers at my family's milk processing plant. I tested the quality and measured the quantity of butterfat in each farmer's can of cream. I then paid him or her accordingly. Policemen, school administrators, farmers, and most of the other citizens I interviewed were friendly and cooperative because we were all western Oklahomans and most knew my family. Some few, however, viewed me with suspicion and could never decide whose "side" I was on. Several individuals informed me that any information about the Indians in Hammon should come from the white community. I was also repeatedly cautioned to "leave those Indians alone." One white professional man wanted "those humanists and communists who come out of the big university to stay away." Another white official stated accusingly, "OU (Oklahoma University) ruins everybody. They just get people down there and indoctrinate 'em."

My research is divided into two periods. The first is from 1974 to 1978. The second began thirty years later, in 2004, and ended in 2007. When I started, I had two purposes in mind. The first was to research a group of people living in one of the many pockets of poverty scattered across the Great Plains to discover how they coped with the everyday shortage of food, livable housing, and reliable transportation, among other things. The second goal of my research was to learn how family relationships were affected by poverty.

I selected a community of Southern Cheyenne, a logical focus, because all indices of their economic and social well being, in 1974, showed that their struggle to survive was probably more difficult than for any other Indian tribe in Oklahoma. I chose a Southern Cheyenne community in western Oklahoma because of its strong adherence to traditional values, most likely attributable to its geographical and cultural isolation. I also chose this particular group for a practical reason—its proximity to my childhood home.

The second period of my research focused on expanding my knowledge of local history and learning if educational and economic conditions had improved for the families I had spent so much time with in the seventies. My pressing interest, however, in the most recent period was to learn what had happened to the grandmothers, their children, and grandchildren with the passing of time. This information could only be obtained by conducting additional interviews with family members and the few old family friends who were still living and who were now in their eighties and nineties. So in 2004, I returned to the Hammon community.

Most of the information that I obtained from the Cheyenne, in the years 1974 to 1978, and 2004 to 2007, came from casual conversations rather than formal interviews. I used a tape recorder part of the time, but in general, I found that many Cheyenne were inhibited when I did. With non-Indians the tape recorder was not an obstacle. White individuals in general were relaxed and anxious to express their opinions of Indians, but with the Indians I was always aware that some comments reached my ears that would have been withheld in a formal, tape-recorded interview.

This study is based mostly on personal information derived from conversations and interviews of a generation of Cheyennes now deceased. All of the persons in this book are real. I have identified most of the Cheyenne and white persons in the text by name. In a few cases I have simply identified the person who gave me information by a general term, i.e., granddaughter, postman, doctor, son. All quotes in the book have been recorded by pen or tape, and are as accurately transcribed in the exact words of the speaker as possible.

In spite of the fact that most of the people I met and interviewed were related to each other, at least in some distant way, they were a diverse group. Disagreements of long standing had factionalized them into two main groups, a traditional group that wanted no change in anything and a progressive group that campaigned for change in a number of areas. One important issue over which they disagreed was education and the kind of school their children and grandchildren should attend.

I gathered information from men, women, children, the old, and the young of both factions. Even though the primary focus of this research is women, I have included many quotes and pictures of men because they are as essential to this study as are the women. Women do not live in isolation. Their roles are defined by men's roles in the same manner that men's roles are defined by the women of this study.

These family histories are especially helpful for understanding the dynamics of power and authority in individual families. A relatively unused medium in anthropology, the family history is often met with distrust because of its highly subjective nature, but I have chosen to use it because it adds an important humanizing dimension to the overall study and allows insight into cultural and gender behavior.

In 1974 my first task was to collect information from each domestic network and interview as many family members as was practical. I began to compile a list of persons in each house, but after several weeks I was forced to abandon that plan because Cheyennes were constantly moving from one house to another. Some left the community temporarily because they were visiting or looking for work, and some moved out permanently. The most likely persons to remain in the community on a full-time basis were those who headed the households, male and female. Using the telephone directory to find names and addresses was not an option because, with the exception of one or two families, none of the Indian population had telephones. Instead I enlisted the help of the water-meter reader, Bill Miller, a non-Indian who knew all of the families, relatives, children, and even where on a particular day or night a family member might have eaten dinner or spent the night.

As I listened to Indian and white stories of hardship, discrimination, and prejudice, I realized that only a small amount of progress had occurred from 1978 to 2006. My greatest concern was an increase in the number of Cheyennes with advanced cases of diabetes. In education, some progress had been made, but a great deal more was needed. In 1976 only five Cheyennes attended the high school, but twice that many were attending in 2004. Also in the summer and the fall of 2005, a few more Cheyennes were employed. The important event was the decision by a vote of the people to allow the operation of casinos by various tribes on tribal lands. The Cheyennes operated two that provided important money supplements for tribal members below the poverty line. Families were still somewhat unstable, because poverty was cruel and deep, but the situation was improving, although slowly.

❧

In 1974 the community of Cheyennes lived in a total of thirty-nine households of constantly changing membership. Large families most frequently were headed by a strong senior mother, or grandmother, and if the grandmother lived in the house or nearby, her role was considerable. This was especially true if there were no resident adult males in the vicinity. However, the older woman's role was somewhat diminished if her physical and mental capacities were in a weakened state.

Three decades passed, and in 2004 I returned to the Bethel Mennonite Cemetery northeast of Hammon. Sadly, all of the men and women of the oldest generation in 1974, with the exception of Emma Lou Standing Water Hart, were now deceased, and many of their children and grandchildren had also died. I reflected on the lives of the Southern Cheyenne grandmothers of that oldest generation—Anna, Martha, Vinnie, Lillie, Emma Lou, and Cornstalk. In the quiet of the afternoon, they were all at peace. The diminishing legibility of some of their grave markers will soon make identification impossible, but this illegibility does not concern traditional Cheyennes because they have a long entrenched avoidance of having anything to do with the dead. The oblivion to which these Cheyenne grandmothers have been committed is wrenching to me for in life they were true pillars of strength and storehouses of resources for their families and the entire Cheyenne community.

This book tells the personal stories of six multi-generational families: 1) to illustrate how deeply entrenched poverty is, and 2) to show how poverty affects the interrelationships in individual families. The material covers the four-generation family of Anna Hawk who was born at the turn of the century and had thirteen great-grandchildren. Anna had a wonderful sense of humor that served as a survival mechanism and helped her cope with everyday disappointments and hardships of living in abject poverty. Anna's friend, Martha Fingernail, was also a great-grandmother who, with her husband, Pete Fingernail, lived in the White Shield camp on the Washita River until 1968 where they raised five daughters and one son, all of whom, incidentally, contracted diabetes.

The history of Lillie Elk River Hayes, a great-grandmother, is primarily about her daughter Cootsie, son-in-law Louis Littleman, and granddaughter, Irene Miles. Lillie grew up in a traditional Cheyenne family and lived in a tepee on the banks of the Washita River for the greater part of her life. Vinnie Hoffman was the owner of the largest amount of land and mineral rights in the community. A generous person, Vinnie shared all she had with anyone who needed help. Another Cheyenne grandmother, who was a model for younger grandmothers, was Anna Reynolds Cornstalk Hart, Tepee Maker. Born in 1876, she was one of the oldest Indian women in the community. Her husband, John Peak, was a peace chief and a priest in the Native American Church. The sixth grandmother is Emma Lou Standing Water Hart. Emma Lou married Lawrence Hart's brother, Alvin, who made the military service his career. Alvin was given a medical discharge for a heart condition, and the couple moved back to Hammon with their eight children.

The family histories are followed by discussions of economics, religion, and education, all of which have played important parts in shaping the present day form of the family.

In Part Four the customs and reciprocal aspects of marriage in earlier times are compared with those of today. It examines power and authority relationships in the family, the spacing of children, crisis fosterage, and child shifting. The importance of the strong ethic of sharing is detailed, and the powwow is explained as a totally altruistic exchange of money and goods. Structural changes in the cultural patterns of the Cheyenne family from 1875 to 2006 have placed more responsibility on the oldest woman in the house. The strategies Cheyenne women employ to enable the family to survive in the current world of poverty and prejudice are summarily discussed, and finally an assessment of the future of the grandmother's role concludes the study.

This is a book of memories, the memories of Cheyenne men and women who found themselves at the beginning of the twentieth century stripped of their economic base, political structure, and spiritual heritage. Indians were believed to be inferior and not worthy of fair treatment. In spite of widespread prejudice and incredible economic disadvantages, the Cheyenne have learned and are learning to cope with an unwelcoming world, primarily through family.

Acknowledgements

I have incurred many personal debts in the preparation of this manuscript. I am especially indebted to the Cheyennes who so willingly answered my questions and shared with me stories of their many struggles, joys, and heartbreaks. They are the most important persons in the book. Among the many who touched my life, in particular, were members of the Hawk family, Anna and her grandchildren, Freeman and Teresa; the Hoffman family, Vinnie, Fred, and Kathryn; the Elk River family, Lillie, Louis and Cootsie Littleman, Irene and Harvey Miles; and the Fingernail family, Martha, Pete, Martin, Tonita, and Joyce; Emma Lou Standing Water Hart, Emma Lou Standing Water Brewer, Joe Osage, and Lawrence and Betty Hart.

Persons who were not Cheyenne but were especially helpful were Judy Jordan, Jan Malone, Patt Hodge, Eldon Payne, and Bill Miller. Jack Haley at the Western History Collections at the University of Oklahoma Libraries and Chester Cowen at the Oklahoma Historical Society, were particularly helpful in finding photographs.

The person who helped most was Max Malone, the pastor of the Indian Baptist Church in Hammon from 1974 to 1978. In the last two months before his death in 2005, he reread this manuscript and recommended some additions. He not only was remarkably perceptive, he also had an uncanny ability to recall details of local history. He knew who had been married and to whom going back many generations. Unfortunately he succumbed to acute leukemia before the study was finished. I am exceptionally fortunate to have been under the tutelage of Professor Bill Bittle (since deceased) at the University of Oklahoma who guided me to the study of Plains Indians that he knew and loved so well. I also am indebted to Victoria Hyde for the map and to Wanda Queenan for her excellent photographs.

Illustrations

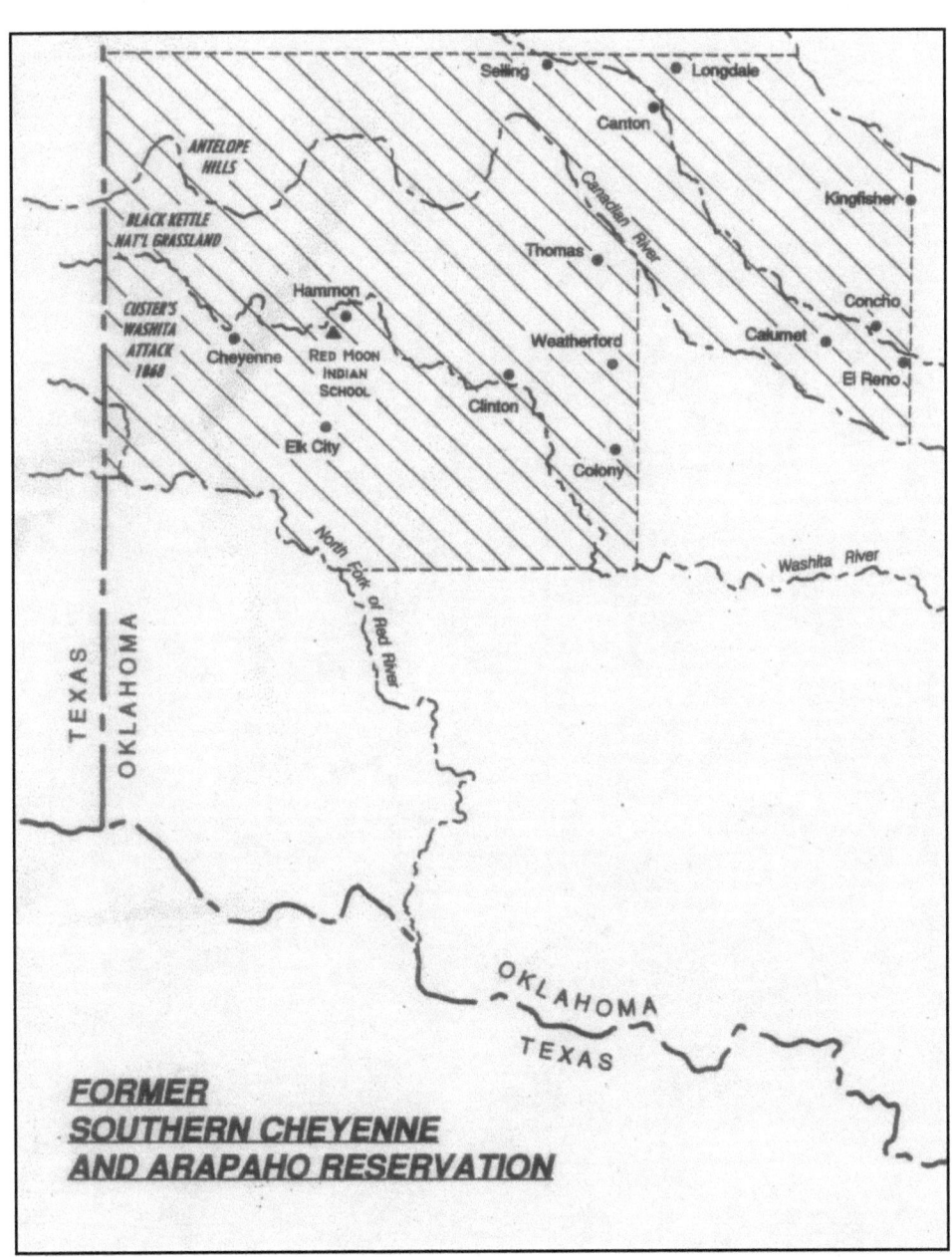

Selling •   • Longdale

Canton •

ANTELOPE
HILLS

Canadian River

Kingfisher •

BLACK KETTLE
NAT'L GRASSLAND

Thomas •

CUSTER'S
WASHITA
ATTACK
1868

Hammon
•
RED MOON
INDIAN
SCHOOL

Cheyenne •

Weatherford •

Concho •

Calumet •

El Reno •

Clinton •

Elk City •

Colony •

Washita River

North Fork of Red River

TEXAS

OKLAHOMA

OKLAHOMA

TEXAS

FORMER
SOUTHERN CHEYENNE
AND ARAPAHO RESERVATION

Introduction

The small rural town of Hammon, Oklahoma, located in the westernmost part of what was formerly the Southern Cheyenne–Arapaho Reservation, is the location of the Southern Cheyenne families who are the focus of this study. Most of the resident Cheyenne are directly descended from one or both of two important peace chiefs—Chief Red Moon and Chief White Shield--and almost all are related to every other Cheyenne in the community in some way. Genealogy charts show just how interrelated the Hammon Cheyennes are despite a tribal prohibition on relatives marrying other relatives.

Today, in 2008, the town of Hammon is more isolated than it was during the oil boom years of the early twentieth century when it could boast a railroad and a more diversified economy. The revival of area oil production in 2002 has strengthened the regional economy, but not measurably. The oil companies, many headquartered out of the state, often bring their own workers and are not very promising as local employers. The labor force for the oil industry usually rents or buys houses in nearby Elk City and no extra housing is available in Hammon, so Hammon Indians only benefit marginally.

The economy today is based almost entirely on agriculture and ranching with dairy and beef cattle ranking first in importance; wheat, second; and alfalfa and cotton, third and fourth (USDA 2002). The harsh growing climate, caused by extreme heat and cold with high wind velocities, unpredictable rainfall, and early mismanagement of the soil, has resulted in excessive erosion of topsoil. Now the trend to large-scale mechanized and irrigated farming has meant the slow demise of small subsistence farms and a greater concentration of land in the hands of a few.

One of the many concerns in the area is the decrease in the town's population, which dropped from 677 in 1975, one year after this study began, to 654 by 2004. During the same period, the total population of the Southern Cheyenne, who constitute approximately thirty-seven percent of the total number of people in the town, has increased. Roger Mills County, where Hammon is located, has lost significant overall population in recent years. Of Oklahoma's seventy-seven counties, Roger Mills County is depopulating at the second highest rate in the state. From January 1990 to January 2000, the total population, whites and Indians, in Roger Mills County declined 17.1 percent, but the American Indian population in the same county increased 7.1 percent (USDOC 36(2) 3–5, 521–523). These numbers, although based on government statistics and loosely confirmed by a house-to-house poll, have by my estimate an estimated error range of five to six percent due to the volatility of the population, but the trends are apparent.

Because of its rather restricted economic base, Hammon provides few job opportunities for anyone whether white or Cheyenne. The most striking feature of the community is the almost sole monopolization of economic opportunities by the white population. Indians are chronically under- and unemployed. During the winter months their employment is almost nonexistent. For the entire tribe unemployment is sixty-six percent, but in Hammon, particularly in the winter months, it can rise as high as ninety percent as agricultural work opportunities disappear (*DO* May 9, 2004). Although Cheyenne economic and social isolation improved considerably when the Cheyenne moved from tepees on the banks of the Washita River, to frame houses in the town, their standard of living remained very low.

Approximately half of the Cheyenne domestic groups, or households, are multi-generational with three, and sometimes four, generations in one household, and if a senior woman, or grandmother, lives there also, she is likely to be the recognized head of the family for three reasons: (1) Indian women on average live longer than men, so there are more of them, (2) more Hammon Cheyenne men than women migrate out of the community looking for employment (women are at home taking care of the children or working locally); and (3) the Cheyenne show a great deal of respect for the elderly. Since the grandmother, is likely to be the oldest woman in the domestic group, she commands much respect from her family and her community.

As I spent time with the different family members in the Cheyenne community observing how they related to each other, it became apparent that the grandmother, or senior mother, in particular, had an exceedingly important role in each of the six family units that received concentrated research. The pattern varied somewhat from one family to another, but in general, the family members regarded the grandmother as the prime authority and valued her wisdom. Even in households that had a resident father or husband, the grandmother was still, more often than not, the power center.

A proliferation of research studies in the 1950s and 1960s focused on the socio-economic characteristics of typical black family structures in the Caribbean and Latin America areas. A wide range of scholars contributed to these studies that are based on fieldwork among blacks living in small, rural communities or urban neighborhoods. All of them emphasized the ubiquity of mother–centered families. R.T. Smith (1996: 38–57) who did field work in British Guiana, coined the word matrifocal to describe the family that centers on the mother–child relationship. The term translates as mother focused, one of the stages in the developing family.

Today most individuals are born into a nuclear family or a single parent family and progress through several different family stages in a lifetime. The birth of the first child marks the beginning of the child rearing stage and bonding between mother and child. As the mother–child bond strengthens, the husband–wife bond weakens, and child rearing becomes the most important activity of the household. The husband easily becomes marginal and either disappears from the home for increasing amounts of time or spatially segregates himself in his home or compound. This is most likely to occur if the husband in his work world and the wife in her domestic world never cross over into the other's territory (Ibid: 54).

A similar family organization outside the Caribbean area is found in England and described by Elizabeth Bott in *Family and Social Networks*

(1968: 69). The same segregated relationships of husband and wife are present in extended families, with a core nucleus of grandmother, her daughters, her daughter's daughters, and her sisters, all of whom sometimes see each other or work together all day long. Cheyenne women's relationships are equally as intense and distinctive as those in England that Bott declares "warrant the term organized group or cluster of female relatives." She noticed that whenever there were no particular economic advantages to be gained by affiliation with paternal relatives, and whenever two or three generations of mothers and daughters were living in the same place at the same time, a bilateral kinship system would likely develop a matrilateral stress; that is, a greater proportion of kinship and descent would occur in the female line instead of the male line. Groups composed of sets of mothers and daughters could form within networks of kin, although "they have no structural continuity. They dissolve soon after the focal grandmother dies or if its members separate from one another." In family studies in Java, Hildred Geertz (1961: 74) stressed the importance of the grandmother's capability to control deviant or lax behavior of family members. On this point the Cheyenne grandmothers are challenged almost daily on two very important issues: (1) reducing alcohol consumption in their families, and (2) convincing their children of the importance of education.

In grandmother focused societies the grandmother is granted affection and loyalty from family members, manifest by frequent mutual aid and high social interaction. Grandmother oriented can apply to families or societies. Geertz states that the nuclear family will be mother focused if the woman has more authority, influence, and responsibility than her husband, and at the same time receives more loyalty and affection. The kindred are mother focused if the persons of greatest influence are women, and the relationships of greatest solidarity are those between women, or those between persons linked by a woman. Relationships with the least amount of influence are those between men or between persons related through men (Ibid.).

The socio-cultural black family structures in Haiti (Bastien); Trinidad (M.J. and F.S. Herskovits 1952); Mexico (Chinas 1973, Stephen 2005); Guatemala (Solien 1960); Jamaica (Davenport 1961); British Guiana (R.T Smith 1956); and the United States (Stack 1975) are remarkably similar. Can this be attributed to borrowed culture? To inherited culture? Or a family structure that is shaped mostly by the environment? Latin America and the Caribbean experienced a similar sequence of historical events. Both were areas of colonization and European power domination, and both showed a correlation between low social status in a stratified society and a type of family system in which men seem to lack importance (R.T. Smith, 1996: 22).

A cross-cultural perspective finds matrifocality in a variety of social and economic contexts. Most tend to be concentrated in societies that have a low sex ratio (a low proportion of men to women as the Cheyenne community has). Other explanations tied to the low sex ratio are: high unemployment and underemployment, itinerate labor markets, military service, and an inordinate amount of time spent by men in recreation or survival hunting. Matrifocality is generally concentrated in poor societies, but matrifocal families do occur among middle and upper class families if the right circumstances present themselves.

In this study the appropriateness of the term matrifocal or grandmother-focused to describe the Hammon Cheyenne with and without a husband/father is based largely on extensive interviews with members of the six extended families selected. Each of them is headed by a grandmother. These grandmothers emerge as the sustainers of Cheyenne culture and family relationships. They have assumed primary responsibility for passing knowledge of plant and herbal remedies, beading skills, preparations of native foods, locations of sacred places and of nature spirits, burial preparations, details of tribal celebrations, dances, songs, and the fundamentals of tribal law to the younger generations.

Grandmothers, as well as grandfathers, are especially treasured for their ability to recall the adventure stories of battles and raiding expeditions, animal stories, ghost stories, and other adventures. In their strong oral tradition many can vividly recount the extraordinary events of their ancestral past. Many also remember the trickster stories that are valued not only for their pedagogical content, but also for their ability to make people laugh. These stories promote an enduring pride in being Cheyenne. In this study, grandmother-centered applies to those families in which the oldest woman is the actual center of power and authority regardless of whether an adult male is physically present. Grandmothers are the sustainers of strength in the Cheyenne family and inspire the pride and charity that help sustain community.

All six grandmothers in this study were children or mothers in nuclear families at one time in their lives, and as they matured and went through life's stages, they became vital parts of other kinds of families. Five of the oldest grandmothers were widows when I first interviewed them, and the husband of the remaining one died shortly after my interview with both of them in the 1970s.

In pre-contact times Indian women had a great deal of power and influence, so we should not be too surprised to find a central kin role for them after contact. Although the daily lives of Indian women differed from tribe to tribe, their lifestyles generally exhibited a great deal more independence and security than those of white women of that period. Not only did some Indian women vote long before women in industrialized societies, but they also owned property (Hudson 1976: 312–313).

Women, particularly in the Plains area, where the exigencies of the environment demanded much flexibility in responsibilities and sexual roles, women, unlike the Bott study women, were on an equal footing with men. Throughout the Plains tribes, men held the key political and religious leadership roles, but women had considerable influence and power, particularly in the domestic area. Given the unpredictability of daily life, the division of labor probably could not have been more equitably drawn. Hunting and raiding kept men away from home for long periods of time, and women became quite skilled in many areas. They were architects and builders of earth lodges, grass houses, and tepees, and when the camp moved, they performed all of the activities required for transporting the group's worldly goods.

Nish ki, the Cheyenne term for grandmother, translates as the biological mother of the biological parent of the grandchild and extends to all female siblings and female spouses of the grandmother's generation. In other words, the biological grandmother and the grandchild's great aunts are called "grandmother," or *nish'ki* in Cheyenne. Being of the oldest generation, the grandmother is often an elder, but not necessarily.

A woman biologically can become a living grandmother in her early thirties, but to be considered an elder, the woman should be at least fifty and have achieved a position of some importance in the tribe or extended family.

The grandmother is respected and loved with few exceptions and being at the power center of her family, she makes most of the critical family economic decisions and taps economic and political resources when needed. She also is considered to be a great source of wisdom. No matter how hard life becomes for the Cheyenne, they can always count on a persevering grandmother to be there with an outstretched hand.

These family stories of Hammon Cheyenne grandmothers herein included are stories of the Indian struggle against poverty and discrimination, but more than that, they are stories of women who are strong-willed and resolute, striving to keep Indian values intact, keep the traditional ceremonies alive, give emotional and financial support to family members and in general to keep the community together and viable. Their stories are compelling.

Part One:

Defeat

Chapter One

THE LOSS OF FREEDOM

The Southern Cheyenne, or Tsistsistas, meaning "the people," are today almost as economically dependent on the government as they were at the time of their confinement to a reservation one hundred forty years ago. The white population's explanation for this failure tends to be couched in demeaning terms: Indians are lazy, Indians are irresponsible, and Indians are alcoholics. These stereotypes in a larger context really mean that Indians have failed economically because they have failed to acculturate and to adopt the white American culture. In spite of several factors that have contributed in some degree to this failure, the simple truth is that whites did not like Indians as they found them and so sought to Americanize them at any cost. The last century of Cheyenne history shows that the cost has been high for both sides, materially as well as psychologically.

From the Cheyenne viewpoint, expressed by Louis Littleman, a former priest in the Native American Church: "You know the Indian used to be honest. Always he was honest. But he took up the white man's ways. The Cheyenne Indians don't cuss. I do because I learned it from the white man. You know the way we feel about the white man is that we don't take his word. We say that the white man has a forked tongue—one part says something, and the other part says something else." Louis chuckled and then he added, "It's all about bein' honest."

The Cheyenne not only lost their economic base, but as a consequence of military defeat and subsequent confinement to a reservation, they also lost all control over their economy and their political, educational, and religious institutions. In becoming wards of the U.S. government, they lost every vestige of their prior self-sufficiency and with it every vestige of self-esteem. These losses, which involved a great deal of personal frustration and demoralization, were to be replaced by the customs and values of white Christian Americans. Whites sought to coerce Indians into the mainstream of white society, but Indians strongly resisted. The government, being totally committed to changing all Cheyenne cultural, social, and political institutions, formulated numerous policies to persuade or force Indians to change to the "white man's way," but with limited success. Most Cheyenne were defiant and held fast to their traditions and institutions.

The Cheyenne failure to adapt to an environment in which they had no autonomy contrasts sharply with their remarkable ability to adapt during the two hundred year period preceding intensive contact with whites. They started their migration from a central Algonquian (the language family to which they belonged) provenance on the northern side of the Great Lakes in 1650. They ended their migration on the Southern Plains in the nineteenth century. Counting all, they successfully made three distinct ecological adaptations.

The earliest Cheyenne habitat, according to migration legends and traditions, was rough, rocky country where the fishing of salmon, trout, whitefish, catfish, sturgeon, pike, and the hunting of small and large game—deer, bear, turkey, beaver, porcupine, and skunk, in particular, were the predominant economic activities (Grinnell 1923, (1): 170–173; Will 1912:68; Moore 1996:14).

In the next period, during their slow migration to the Northern Plains, they adapted to a flat country of sparse trees and tall red grass, where they lived as semi-sedentary horticulturalists in earth-lodge dwellings (Grinnell 1923 1: 3-7). Today their best-known site is the Biesterfeldt site on the Sheyenne River in North Dakota, where approximately seventy lodges with an estimated population of nine hundred people camped from about 1724 to 1790. While there, the Cheyenne acquired the horse and traded for glass beads and metal knives, but apparently did not yet possess the gun. Sometime after they reached the Missouri River farther west, they joined with the Suhtai, another Algonquian-speaking tribe.

Nothing is known of the Suhtai before they reached the Plains. It may be coincidental, but it was at this time that Cheyenne villages registered a sudden, substantial increase in population. Rudolph Petter's (1936) research confirms that the differences in the languages of these two Algonquian-speaking tribes are only dialectic, which probably accounts for the complete assimilation of the two tribes. The Suhtais brought many new customs to the Cheyennes. They introduced the Sun Dance, which was always performed in the Suhtai dialect. They introduced the buffalo, a great tribal fetish that was a source of health and prosperity to the tribe; the Sacred Tepee; and the tribal palladium that afforded sanctuary to fugitives from the law and as a place of safe keeping for persons trying to escape some domestic difficulty.

The joining of the Tsistsistas bands with the four bands of the Suhtai marked the beginning of the Cheyenne nation. The southern group, who called themselves Heviksnipahis, Hisiometanio, and Masikota, and the northern group, known as the Eaters, Omisis, or Wotapio routinely camped at great distances from each other. Their numbers were in constant flux, expanding and contracting with the changing of fortunes (Moore 1996: 159–175).

Chiefs of the largest bands were accorded a great deal of prestige. The ideal way to acquire this prestige was for brothers and sisters of one family to marry brothers and sisters from another family. Multiple marriages prompted lavish giveaways of gifts and strengthened alliances (Ibid.). The Cheyenne sometime in the 1700s allied themselves with the Arapaho, another Plains tribe that had recently split off from the Atsina tribe. The alliance was a wise move because both the Cheyenne and the Arapaho tribes were having a shortage of warriors making them more vulnerable to attack. The alliance strengthened both tribes.

With their arrival on the Southern Plains in the third quarter of the eighteenth century, the Cheyenne began the process of assuming their third mode of existence as full-blown nomadic equestrians. They were living in tepees, raiding for horses, hunting buffalo, gathering berries, and digging root vegetables. It is likely that they hunted small game, when it was available, and practiced horticulture to some degree, but the utilization of the buffalo far outweighed the uses of other foods. By the middle of the nineteenth century they had reached the height of their cultural fluorescence. They were enjoying their days of freedom, the buffalo on which they depended were plentiful, essential trade goods were easy to obtain, and white threats to Indian lands had not yet become a pressing concern (Jablow 1951).

Events took a drastic turn in the 1850s. White encroachment on Cheyenne lands, which began in the early part of the century, accelerated dramatically with the discovery of gold in California in 1849. Thousands of opportunistic gold seekers pushed through the heart of the Plains Indian buffalo range, and white American hunters began the slaughter of the buffalo. In the short span of fifteen years, the buffalo that had furnished most of the Indians' food and shelter had disappeared, and the lucrative market for Indian buffalo robes that had been especially important to the Indians as trade items had collapsed. As white hunters destroyed the mainstay of the Plains Indians, white homesteaders rushed to grab Indian land and to own it as justified by Manifest Destiny, the nineteenth century doctrine that the U.S. had the God-given right and duty to expand and spread its political, economic, and religious influence over the whole of North America. The invaders took what they wanted. In response, the Indians began revenge raids that quickly escalated to battles and finally a full-fledged war. Mistrust fostered by broken promises intensified the conflict.

By the mid-1860s some Cheyenne had become resigned to their fate and were willing to surrender. The U.S. Army promised peace, but many Cheyenne were suspicious, especially after the malicious slaughter of men, women, and children in the Battle of Sand Creek in 1864. Representatives of some of the Cheyenne bands agreed to the terms of the Medicine Lodge treaty in 1867 in which the U.S. government assigned lands in the Cherokee Outlet of Indian Territory (roughly the northwest part of Oklahoma today, excluding the panhandle) to the Southern Cheyenne and Southern Arapaho, although finally they would be restricted to the area south of the Cherokee Outlet.

In the winter of 1868, Black Kettle and various bands of the Cheyenne were migrating south from a location on the northern Plains to a warmer climate, planning to meet other bands in one big encampment. Black Kettle, however, was a peace chief and not very welcome by the warrior societies. When he arrived at the warrior's encampment with his followers, according to Anna Cornstalk Hart (WOHP MJW May 19, 1995), the warriors told Black Kettle that he was not welcome and suggested that he go to another place to camp. So he went several miles west and set up camp. This placed him and his followers isolated some distance from the main group. In so doing, he unsuspectingly had increased his and his followers' vulnerability to an attack. At dawn on November 27, 1868, General George Armstrong Custer staged a surprise attack on Black Kettle's camp that quickly turned into a wholesale massacre of Cheyenne men, women, and children. It became known as the Battle of the Washita (Brill 2001: 311). The survivors of the battle settled in the Hammon area approximately thirty miles east of the battlefield.

Raids and minor skirmishes accelerated. After the Cheyenne defeat at the Battle of Summit Springs in 1869, most of the militant faction of the Cheyenne, the Dog Soldiers, headed north to join the war faction of the Northern Cheyenne in Montana who were still fighting. The remaining Dog Soldiers withdrew and joined the peace faction of the Southern Cheyenne in the South.

The most famous battle was at Adobe Walls in June 1874, when warriors from five Southern Plains tribes decided to attack the white buffalo hunters and traders at the Adobe Walls Trading Post near the present-day city of Amarillo, Texas. At a critical time when the white man's wholesale slaughter of the buffalos threatened the very survival of the Plains Indians, the Indians decided to attack. The two to three hundred Indians thought they were protected from harm by the medicine shirt of a young Comanche prophet who accompanied them. But when given the test, the shirt failed. The Cheyennes and the Comanches lost nine men and had little overall success against the barricaded white defenders. They continued scattered, small attacks, but were driven to resignation to their fate by hunger. They returned to the agency at Concho, I.T. in 1875 (Berthrong 1963: 384–390). Federal agents immediately put thirty-one Indians in leg irons and sent them to prison in Ft. Marion, Florida, without a trial or a hearing.

By 1875 at least twenty Cheyenne camps had been systematically burned and plundered by U.S. troops (Petersen 1971: 26), and the Cheyenne were still raiding to escape starvation. In the wider war, the Cheyenne were divided on the issue of surrender. At the Indian agency, the warriors were in control and would not allow the peace faction to leave the main camp.

General Sheridan was convinced that the Cheyenne were the most formidable of the Southern Plains tribes and if they could be subdued and punished, the backbone of Indian resistance would be crushed (Ibid.). The U.S. Army staged a vigorous campaign against the Cheyennes, and the Southern Cheyenne defenses deteriorated in protracted fighting. The Cheyennes never really had a chance. They were not united, they had insufficient weapons with which to fight, and they could easily be surprised or outmaneuvered by their enemy. The professionally trained army of the United States soldiers was helped by individual Indians serving as scouts. The scouts were valuable advisors because they knew the geography of the area and the likely strategies of other Indian tribes. The Cheyennes fought valiantly but were soon rendered powerless against the superior military force of the United States Army (Mooney 1907: 379–385).

The courage and skill with which the Cheyenne fought to protect their right to lead an autonomous existence on the Plains won them respect from other tribes and whites alike. The decisive U.S. army campaign of 1874–1875 ended with the surrender of 821 Cheyenne on March 6, 1875. By August, the fighting had ended (Berthrong 1963: 400–405).

After achieving the distinction of being one of the last Indian tribes to be subdued by the United States Army, the Southern Cheyenne with their confederates, the Southern Arapaho, were assigned slightly over four million acres of reservation lands in Indian Territory, an area located between the Cimarron and Arkansas Rivers, which today is in northwest Oklahoma.

Chapter Two

RECALCITRANCE

The descendants of the Southern Cheyenne who located in the western part of the Cheyenne–Arapaho Reservation, now northwestern Oklahoma, are the focus of this study. Red Moon, who was married to Sioux Woman, was their main chief. He was the son of Yellow Wolf, the chief of the Hevhaitaneo band who had been killed in the Sand Creek Massacre of 1864.

Red Moon's band of seventy lodges camped in a wide area extending from the Antelope Hills to the Cimarron River in the present western Oklahoma counties of Woodward and Ellis before the surrender of 1875 (Linscheid 1973:13). After the surrender, the Indian Agency at Darlington moved Red Moon's camp to a Washita River location, a few miles north of the present town of Hammon, Oklahoma, and also located the camps of White Shield, Howling Water, and Spotted Horse from the eastern reservation area to the location of Red Moon's camp on the Washita River in the west (Petter 1936:45).

The Cheyenne in Red Moon's camp on the Washita from the beginning of the reservation period were the most active opponents to the changes imposed by the U.S. government. They balked at and actively contested every government policy that affected them. The government repeatedly formulated and reformulated policies aimed at developing economic independence for them, but the policies largely failed because they ignored basic economic principles and lacked understanding.

9

Indians reacted by resisting because they found change to the white way undesirable and often impossible.

Chief Red Moon, Photo by H.J. Stevenson, El Reno, O.T. and his band were the main occupants of the Washita River location of the western section of the Cheyenne–Arapaho Reservation. Photo no. 3751. Courtesy, Research Division of the Oklahoma Historical Society.

Being located in remote and isolated camps allowed them to protest and be successful in resisting change. The government viewed agriculture along with animal husbandry as the most promising line of work for Indians, hoping for enough success to allow Indians to end their dependency on government rations. Through education, Christianization, and the individual prodding by Indian agents, Indians were to be gently coerced to change from hunter to farmer.

Some Cheyenne in the Red Moon district made an earnest effort to farm, but others held fast to their old habits of camp life and refused to change. Cheyennes who attempted to plant crops or raise cattle were often deterred by members of the Cheyenne Soldier Societies, who destroyed crops and plundered cattle herds to prevent others from cooperating with the U.S. government (Berthrong 1976: 103-104).

When an agricultural economy failed to materialize on communal reservation lands, the government's next policy to bring about economic independence of Indians was to transform them into individual farmers. So they decided to allot Indian land in severalty and create surplus reservation land for white settlement, an action that would shrink the original 4,000,000 acres to 529,682 acres. An important provision of the Medicine Lodge Treaty of 1867 prohibited Cheyennes and Arapahos from ceding any more allotted land after 1867 unless approved and signed by seventy-five percent of the adult males in the two tribes (Ibid.).

Negotiations between the U.S. government representatives and the Southern Cheyenne and Arapaho chiefs broke down repeatedly, but the reality was that the white homesteaders wanted Indian land, and the Cheyenne and Arapaho were forced to acquiesce. The Dawes Act of 1887 allotting Indian land in severalty was then applied to the Southern Cheyenne in March 1891, even though many Cheyenne had refused to sign the agreement. Of those who did, a large number were males under the age of twenty-one or women, two groups who did not have the right to vote, but whose signatures were solicited and then counted dubiously by the U.S. agent. Agent Ashley was then able to produce the seventy-five percent of adult Cheyenne and Arapaho signatures required by the Medicine Lodge Treaty to cede the Indian land. Agent Ashley's figures were also dubious because the rate of mortality from tuberculosis, venereal disease, pneumonia, and other contagious diseases had been rising rapidly in the last half of the nineteenth century, and the birth rate declining (Ibid.165–168).

The Southern Cheyenne in the Red Moon district were the most outspoken opponents of the allotment decision. They contested the validity of the cession agreement and charged that the signatures were obtained fraudulently, but to no avail. Seven-eighths of their reservation land was seized for settlement by non-Indians, and the remaining eighth divided into allotments for the Cheyenne and Arapaho tribes. The Hammon Cheyennes refused to accept their allotments of one hundred sixty acres each or to take any of the one and one half million dollars that was payment for ceded lands (Ibid. 166-170). After the cession, the bands of Red Moon, White Shield, and Spotted Horse attempted to force white settlers to leave what they considered to be fraudulent claims (RCIA 1892: 375).

Although every adult Cheyenne was given an allotment, few attempted to farm. Of those who did, most gave up, but a few others, one of whom was Homer Hart, not only continued to farm, but shared some of his farming machinery with neighbors who did not have any.

Not to be deterred by increasing failures, the government then attempted to teach Indians agricultural skills by using Indian teachers. Anna Hawk recalled, "My father, he was an assistant farmer. He helped everybody. He showed Indians how to plant. He showed them how to raise crops. Every Indian went to my father for help. They all were good farmers when he teach them." But she remembered also that her father had considerable difficulty growing crops on his own farm because "there was never any money for machines, the soil was bad, and the rain never came at the right time." Her father was more successful at raising animals. Some of Anna's fondest memories were of the many hours she had spent riding horses with her father as he traveled to care for Cheyenne cows, horses, and hogs.

Martha Fingernail remembered that her family quit farming after her husband's sister died, but "it was too hard anyway." The mandated transition to farming required too much change for a nomadic group of people and did not realistically take into account the great cultural and historical differences between Cheyenne and whites. As nomadic hunters, the Cheyenne were mobile and lived and worked cooperatively. As agriculturalists, they were expected to be sedentary and live and work individually. They were not adequately informed nor technically prepared for managing farms. Not only did they lack the regimentation necessary for farming, they could not recover from a bad crop year and survive. More importantly, they had no desire to be farmers.

Hostility, fear, and suspicion have characterized Indian–white relations since contact. Beginning in the late nineteenth century, Indians regarded whites as failing to extend courtesy, justice, fair dealing, and friendliness to them, and the pervasive belief of whites was that Indians were inferior, a belief that has clouded every decision that affects Indians. In the early allotment years, the antipathy of whites toward Indians translated into consistently unfair treatment in their local legal system. White juries and judges did not apply the law equally to Indians and whites and considered victimization of Indians justifiable (Berthrong 1976: 185–190).

Sioux Woman was the wife of Red Moon. Photo c. 1895– 1901. Photo no. 35
Courtesy, Research Division of the Oklahoma Historical Society.

Whites were able to take advantage of Indians, in great part, because Indians misunderstood their unique status in two important areas. First, although Indians were entitled to vote, they were denied that right on numerous occasions. One such vote they were denied in the early part of the century was on the critical issue of open range in Roger Mills County. The consequences were disastrous for Indians when open range was approved because it essentially gave license to the cattle herds belonging to whites to overrun allotments, thereby causing extensive damage to Indian crops and gardens. The Attorney General subsequently handed down an opinion upholding the Indians' right to vote and their right to be protected against open-range laws, but county authorities chose to ignore it.

Chief Ben White Shield, Age 74, a son of Old Man White Shield and Back Killer at American Indian Exposition, Anadarko, Oklahoma, c.1948. He served as a principal chief for the Cheyenne from 1936 until the year of his death 1967. He and Red Moon were the primary progenitors of the Hammon Cheyennes. Photo by Pierre Tartoué. Courtesy, Research Division of the Oklahoma Historical Society.

Second, although Indians were exempt from taxation on allotments and any personal property acquired by trust funds or money from the federal government, many of them were forced to pay taxes anyway.

Persons failing to pay lost their property, and whites were able to acquire it. Several local Indians told stories about how they or their parents lost property because of a failure to pay taxes. Some of the tax collectors knew that the Indians were being wronged, but in judicial matters Indians never expected to get a fair ruling.

The U.S. government's decision to make individual farmers of the Cheyenne came at a time when subsistence farming by any individual was already giving way to large-scale, single-crop enterprises. Lack of tools, poor soils, and unpredictable climatic conditions hindered individual cultivation of the soil. Crop yields were so low that even long time efficient white farmers could not subsist on a quarter section of land. Intensive efforts by missionaries, educators, legislators, and Indian agents to abolish Indian social and religious institutions and inculcate the values and skills of the white farmer brought about surprisingly little change in the western camps of Red Moon, White Shield, and Spotted Horse.

In 1897 Major A. E. Woodson, the Indian agent at Darlington, being distressed by the lack of economic and cultural progress by the most recalcitrant Cheyenne, made a decision to withhold rations and annuity goods (wagons, cooking and heating stoves, lumber, and canvas) from chiefs whose followers still resisted the newly prescribed way of life. Red Moon's, Spotted Horse's, and White Shield's bands were prime targets. To Woodson's dismay, their bands were living in large camps, using peyote, practicing traditional religious ceremonies, using traditional medicine men to cure illness, adhering to the Indian customs of marriage and divorce which included plural wives, continually visiting their neighbors and friends for extended periods of time, and refusing to labor or farm on their allotments. At first the threat of withholding rations had little impact because some of them still had money from payments for ceded land, and many were able to obtain credit for food (Berthrong 1976: 212–214). Finally Woodson's policy of refusing rations and annuities to those who opposed him began to pay off. Eleven out of twenty-three Cheyenne chiefs and all but one Arapaho chief agreed to Woodson's demands, but Red Moon, White Shield, Old Crow, White Horse, Little Big Jake, and Burnt-All-Over, still resisted.

By 1900, the 186 Cheyennes in the westernmost portion of the agency were living in extremely impoverished and crowded conditions. Forty-nine of the families still lived in tepees, with only seven families occupying houses for a part of the year. Families of three to ten people frequently occupied tepees or tents that measured sixteen by fourteen feet (Ibid. 267).

In 1909 the U.S. government cut off funds to the BIA. The desperate level of living conditions in those early years of the century is reflected in the excessively high illness and mortality rates. Extremely cold weather and severe storms during this period usually set off a rash of sickness and death. Influenza, pneumonia, and tuberculosis were the main killers, with young children from one to five and older people being the most frequent victims (RCIA: 1900–1945). The Cheyenne were barely able to maintain a meager subsistence level by hunting small animals and growing vegetables that they dried and preserved. To stimulate the interest of the Indian in farming, the government sponsored a number of fairs for the Cheyenne and Arapaho. They gave a large number of money prizes for the best farm and garden produce, and they asked local experts to speak on various aspects of farming (*HN*: March 31, 1911).

Many Cheyennes planted watermelons, corn, cucumbers, and cantaloupes. Henry Elk River had an especially productive garden and shared with everyone, but also everyone else who could shared with relatives and neighbors so that no one had to go without food. Some fish were available from the river, but no one could fish without a license because as Louis Littleman declared, "The white man said that the fish belonged to the government." Small animals were hunted and the surplus meat dried for later use. The food preservation method of drying enabled food to be kept for consumption year round and added some variety to the government rations that were issued in times of need.

To prevent starvation in those early years, the Cheyenne were permitted to lease their uncultivated lands to white farmers and stockmen, but since almost half of the allotted land had been sold, the land remaining was inadequate to provide enough income for all to survive.

The Cheyenne political organization was particularly troublesome for government officials. In those early years the Cheyenne had three overlapping organizational bodies that were heavily weighted with chiefs or headmen. First, were the ten Cheyenne headmen of the ten Cheyenne bands, the groups of extended families that camped and hunted together. Second, was the tribal council of forty-four chiefs, called the Council of Forty-Four, which served as the backbone of the Cheyenne governing political structure. It had four head chiefs, an executive chief, and thirty-nine councilors who represented the ten bands. Third were the five military societies that all adult men were expected to join, the Dog Soldiers, the Bowstring Soldiers, the Elk Soldiers, the Red Shields, and the Fox Soldiers, each with four little war chiefs and four big war chiefs. Also troublesome for the U.S. authorities was the defiance of the military societies, that operated independently and were inclined to go on enemy expeditions with or without any kind of consensus of the rest of the tribe.

The polit1ical structure of the numerous and independent Cheyenne chiefs had worked very well for the Cheyenne in pre-reservation times, but it was a great source of irritation to U.S. government officials, because it was impossible for the officials to know how to negotiate with such widely scattered authority. Much to the consternation of the BIA, the tribe was not willing to give up any chiefs.

The Secretary of the Interior sought to reduce the number of chiefs by proposing a new organization that would be made up of local representatives who were elected and not appointed. It was called the tribal council and it was established in 1928. All of the important chiefs from the Arapaho and Cheyenne communities were given council positions. The goal of the government in establishing a business committee in addition to the tribal council, was to obtain a balance of power between the two bodies, but by giving the business committee the power to enter into contracts, the government inadvertently made the business committee more powerful than the tribal council. The result was a government with no checks and balances.

Whites soon began to acquire Indian land in great quantities by legal and fraudulent means. Many Indians had to sell their land to whites who had allowed Indians to run up large debts. The only collateral Indians had was their allotment that they did not yet have the legal right to sell. But on the day the Indians were issued a legal document, giving them the right to own a specified piece of land, whites began to collect. It became common practice for bankers and law officers to fine Indians large sums for minor infractions and when the Indians could not pay, the bank or the local judge would seize their property as payment. By 1974, eighty-five percent of Cheyenne and Arapaho allotted lands were no longer in their possession (Ibid. 19).

Discrimination took many forms. Sometimes it was subtle, but at other times quite blatant. Well into the mid-twentieth century a day of Indian labor was sometimes paid for with a case of beer. Even in the late 1950s and early 1960s there were still isolated cases of this practice. Some white farmers, who needed hired hands for the day, would drive into town and pick up the number of workers they needed. When the work was finished, a case of beer or a bottle of liquor was given as payment by some of the farmers. Martha Fingernail who had expected to pay the family utility bill with her husband's wages said with resignation, "There was nothin' the workers could do."

The most disturbing aspect of Cheyenne daily life was the double standard in the legal system. Indians were arrested under conditions and circumstances that whites were not. Excessive brutality was commonly used in the arrest of Indians but only rarely in the case of whites. Racial bias against Indians was frequently voiced by law officers (*CRH* April 26, 1977). Arrest rates in Roger Mills County, the county in which Hammon and Cheyenne are located, provide further evidence of this discrimination.

Roger Mills County had the highest arrest rates for their representation in the population of any group in the state in 1974. Although only 6.6 percent of the county's population was Indian, eighty-nine percent of those arrested in 1974 were Indians (*DO* February 1, 1977). Those figures were compiled at Cheyenne, the county seat, located thirty-five miles west of Hammon and did not include arrests at the Hammon jail. Inexplicably, the jail at Hammon did not keep records of arrests, but law enforcement officers privately estimated that Indians comprised about ninety-five percent of all arrests. Leslie Hawk, who was Anna Hawk's son, confirmed that:

> Indians get harsher treatment than whites. It really just depends on the individuals. But they just accept it because if they don't, it might get worse. Indian values are not like the white man's. The white man only wants to make more money, get ahead. The Indian doesn't care about money. He doesn't compete. He just accepts. That's the way it has always been. The Indian has always accepted how he was treated. The Indian knows no one will speak up for him. It's always better to pay the fine or go to jail because there isn't any trouble that way.

In explaining how Indians have learned to accept a world in which they have few rights and very few privileges, one exasperated Indian man stated, "Everybody has just given up. They've just decided there isn't anything they can do about it."

In 1976 when I visited the police station to ask about Indian arrests, I met Robert Edwards, who was one-half Choctaw Indian. He had been the sheriff in Hammon, but he was dismissed because, he was convinced, he was viewed as being too pro-Indian. "There are two laws in this town—one for the white man and one for the Indian. This town is run like, you wouldn't believe, and the people who run the town like to abuse Indians. They don't really consider them human beings."

A positive aspect of having a local jail, voiced by several people, was that a jail enabled a spouse, parent, grandparent, or friend to sign a complaint against a drinking relative who could then be put in a safe place until sober. From 1974 to 1978, wives, sisters, mothers, fathers, brothers, and even grandmothers often looked to the jail to solve their problem. The offending prisoner then had to pay a twenty-dollar fine that he could "work off" at four dollars per day doing the equivalency of yard work.

In today's world, the four-dollar fine has increased dramatically to a one hundred thirty dollar fine. Most of the tickets are issued on

19

or near the two intersecting highways rather than some place in town because the highway intersection is more dangerous. The Hammon police station does not keep records, but it did have copies of one hundred seventy tickets that the policeman had written from September to the last of February, which seems a lot for the low population. In 2007 Hammon had one policeman and the county of Roger Mills had one deputy sheriff.

The Cheyenne drafted a constitution and by-laws that were approved by the council May 25, 1929, by the Secretary of the Interior, August 25, 1937, and by the tribe one month later. The ratification of the constitution and by-laws accomplished two important tribal needs: (1) It set new criteria for membership in the Cheyenne–Arapaho Tribe, and (2) it created and gave responsibilities to two governing bodies, the newly established business committee of elected members and the tribal council that was made up of all male and female enrolled tribal members, eighteen years or older.

An amendment passed in 1959 changed membership criteria for Cheyennes born after 1959. The new legislation required members to have at least one-fourth Cheyenne and/or Arapaho blood quantum, and second, have at least one parent enrolled in the Cheyenne and Arapaho Tribe.

A new constitution was drafted in 1975 for the purpose of putting into operation a system of checks and balances. However, it failed to provide a set of guidelines for the spending of tribal money. The failure to provide some means of oversight of expenditures—no checks and balances, has led to considerable abuse.

In the early allotment years when Indians were particularly obstinate, education was the one area in which whites made some inroads. After Red Moon and White Shield said that they would send their children to school only if school buildings were constructed near their western camps, government officials authorized a boarding school near Hammon. The school upon which construction was started in 1894, opened in 1897. Although no students attended the first year, in 1898, thirty-two students from Red Moon's and White Shield's bands were enrolled (RCIA 1897–1898).

The Cheyenne persistence in continuing the Indian way of life was irritating to many whites and government officials. To others, it was a mere curiosity. An event in Red Moon's camp in 1934 (*ECDN* April 4, 6, 8, 1934) illustrates the great gulf between Indian culture and white culture, and the Indian's resourcefulness in solving their ever-present scarcity of food.

One day early in April of 1934, the wife of Heap-of-Crows had a vision of a coming flood. She warned all of the Cheyenne families camped on the riverbanks of the impending danger. She also warned a number of whites who either did not understand the possible danger or chose to ignore her. On April 3, 1934, in less than twenty-three hours a devastating downpour of 13.76 inches fell on the upper Washita River watershed near Cheyenne, a neighboring town about thirty-five miles west of Hammon. The Washita River, swollen beyond its banks roared down the one-half to three-quarter-mile wide river valley with such volume that by midnight the river had reached flood stage for a distance of seventy-five miles.

The area where Cheyennes had been camped just minutes earlier was engulfed. Without warning a wall of water estimated by survivors to be four or five feet high swept a number of white persons and animals into the river. The death toll from drowning was 17 white persons, 133 cows, 23 horses, 26 calves, and 560 chickens. But every Indian who lived on the riverbank, escaped the treacherous waters. Judge Beavers, one of the Indians in White Shield's camp, estimated that the waters began to rise about 12:30 a.m. setting off an Indian panic to evacuate and move every tepee and tent from the riverbank. All endangered families hurriedly moved to higher ground, a move that took about fifteen minutes. Suddenly and without warning, a wall of water four to five feet high thundered through the valley. One hour later the water in the river channel was forty feet deep.

As the waters began to ebb, the Cheyenne spotted the carcasses of the dead cows and hogs and quickly laid claim to as many as they could carry to a butchering spot. They first cut the animal down the middle and then cut each half into quarters. They sliced each quarter into thin strips and hung them in the sun to dry on wires, fences, and drying racks constructed from tree limbs. Blowout Scabby, the 104-year old Cheyenne great great-grandmother, said that the jerked beef would "keep for three months and be almost as good as buffalo."

When the State Health Commission heard that the Indians were eating the drowned cows' meat, they were at loose ends as to how to stop the practice. They finally sent crews to gather and guard the remaining dead animals to keep the Indians from adding to their meat supply. The incident was covered in three issues of the local newspaper, piquing the curiosity of hundreds of outsiders who formed long lines to drive by to see the spectacle.

Cheyennes were amused at the authorities' reaction and considered their windfall food supply cause for a celebration. They gathered on blankets and tarpaulins to pass the pipe and jerk the beef while the sightseers gawked at them. Anna Hawk recalled, "It was like a party. That meat's real good, and we had enough to last for a long time. It was pretty funny seein' everybody drive by and take our pictures. Some were tryin' to stop us. What they didn't know is that Cheyennes have been doin' that for years and nobody ever got sick."

Although the Cheyenne escaped with their lives, there was still the reality that many of the family possessions-ceremonial clothing, tools, foodstuffs, bed clothing, weapons, tepees and special items had been swept away. Martha Fingernail lamented that they had to start all over again, and it had taken several years to recover.

The Washita River flood and the Battle of the Washita are two landmark events in Hammon Cheyenne history. Both are dramatic events that threatened death, one by nature, the other by technology. The Cheyenne won the battle against the flood, but lost it against technology.

In 1934 the Indian Reorganization Act was passed that gave Indians the freedom to draft a constitution and govern themselves, but not much happened because not every tribe understood what was involved. The bill authorized tribes to take over financial and legal administration through contractual arrangements with the agencies that previously administered them--law enforcement, road maintenance, forestry, health services: mental health, dental care, hospitals and clinics. In addition the Act stipulated that tribal contractors were to receive the same amount of funding that HHS would have received. The legislation was badly needed to help the tribes begin to climb out of their every day misery.

Several decades passed before the government succeeded in coaxing even a few Cheyennes to move from the river camp to their allotments, but the government's goal was virtually unattainable for two reasons. First, with the passing of each decade the Hammon Cheyenne were progressively losing land on which to move. Second, the Cheyenne had no desire to move. They liked living together and having mobility. Many moved frequently from their camping grounds to allotments (either their own or someone else's), or would camp out at the school area where one or more of their children attended school and then return to their camps. Some moved in with friends or relatives, while others took tents or tepees with them for the purpose of joining any tribal campout like a powwow or fair. They camped out for a period of a few days to as much as several weeks. Ordinarily they arrived a couple of days before and remained for several days to a week after festivities.

Several decades after the battle on the Washita, skeletal remains began to gradually be unearthed in or near the Washita battleground. Knowing that these probably belonged to some of the Cheyenne victims of the Battle on the Washita, Cheyennes began reburying the remains in special ceremonies as the remains were discovered.

On a November weekend in 1930, sixty-two years after the battle, a commemoration of Black Kettle and his followers was held on the Washita battleground. Bones of the Unknown Soldier were reburied with Jacob Runner, Chief Magpie, Yellow Eyes, Philip White Shield, and John Otterby, serving as pallbearers. Left Hand and Little Beaver were participants (Brill 2002).

Another commemoration of Black Kettle and his followers was planned to celebrate the one-hundredth anniversary of the battle along with a reenactment of that battle. When the time arrived to reenact that battle, the California group, called the Grandsons of the Seventh Cavalry, arrived on the scene dressed in authentic red uniforms that were exact replicas of the ones worn by U.S. troops in 1868. The Cheyenne were unnerved as the Californians marched through the village to the marching tune of "Garry Owen," and shooting blank cartridges into the air.

According to Lawrence Hart, "The events became all too real. Deep feelings of hostility erupted." After many tense moments, Lawrence was asked by the Cheyenne peace chiefs to drape a prized woolen blanket over the shoulders of the captain of the Seventh Cavalry, as a gesture of peace. Lawrence was horrified at the idea of honoring the "enemy," but he could not refuse to do what the elder peace chiefs had requested, so with trembling hands, he proceeded with the placement of the blanket on the captain's shoulders. He realized as he stepped back, that his gesture had sparked a very emotional reconciliation. In a quick look around the group there was not a dry eye among them. "The old peace chiefs were very wise," commented Hart (2005).

The Battle of the Washita was recently commemorated by the Oklahoma Historical Society with the building of a museum on the battleground site.

The outbreak of World War I brought a desperately needed economic boost to the impoverished Cheyenne community. Military service provided respectable employment, a living wage, and an opportunity to travel. The war also brought an opportunity for Indians to show their patriotism. Almost every able-bodied man volunteered and some women did also. Nationwide nearly seventeen thousand American Indians served in World War I. Three-fourths of them were volunteers. The war brought a boost to the Cheyenne economy, not only with military service, but also with new and expanded industries servicing the military. Approximately fifty thousand native people left their home area between 1941 and 1945 to work in the expanded wartime industries.

During all the wars, World War I, World War II, the Vietnam and Persian Gulf Wars, Cheyenne warriors were fearless, ferocious, and brave. They carried war medicines, painted their faces, scalped the enemy, and performed war rituals. All who fought, and especially those who were decorated, achieved a high status in the tribe, and many joined the Dog Soldiers, (a Cheyenne military society known for its independence and fierceness) when they returned to the tribe.

Indian participation in the military led to a real turning point in the government's attitude toward Indians and prompted the passing of important legislation that increased their well-being. First, citizenship was offered to all returning service men in 1919 and later to all American Indians in 1924. Second, in 1934 the Self-Determination Act gave American Indians civic and cultural rights, among them the right to manage their own affairs and practice their native religion. The changes were not realized for many years because a large amount of time was required to inform tribes about the legislation, and many tribes were unable to understand the legislation and the legislative process.

During World War I, mothers who had lost a son in the war, became "Gold Star Mothers," and all mothers who had a son in the military organized the Cheyenne War Mothers. The mothers celebrated with powwows to raise money for the soldiers, and they made shawls for themselves decorated with the name, the military achievements, and rank of their sons. All of this activity reinforced traditional men's roles in the defunct warrior societies and nirvana of the past.

Patriotism surged as World War II became a reality. More than twenty-five thousand American Indians served in the military forces and were awarded over two hundred medals and citations. The percentage of American Indian participation in relation to their total population was higher than for any other ethnic group represented, including Anglo-Americans. American Indians invested over seventeen million dollars in war bonds and furnished a great amount of food, money, agricultural products, and reservation lands for military bases (Hale 1992).

At social events they danced as a group counter-clockwise, the opposite way from the other dancers (Meadows 1999: 390–391). Patriotic rallies, celebrations, war bond rallies, and dedication powwows were frequent and served to unite the tribe again. During the war nearly fifty thousand Indians left their homes for military service and wartime employment in the larger cities. After the war some stayed in the cities, but others came back to Hammon even though postwar employment was almost nonexistent, especially in the small towns of Oklahoma. So Indians, in the 1950s, were relocated in urban areas under the government's Relocation Act. The move was successful for some, but not for others, who opted to return to Hammon, in spite of having little chance of finding a job (Ibid.).

In approximately 1958 families began to move out of the camp on the Washita River in significant numbers, one family at a time, into the town of Hammon. In 1968 when each Cheyenne received a twenty-three hundred dollar check from the government as a settlement for past grievances, most of the remaining Cheyenne bought houses in Hammon to own individually or as part of a group. The camp numbers thinned, and Old Ben White Shield finally acquiesced. He was the last Cheyenne to move into town in 1968.

Reburial of the Unknown Soldier of the Battle of the Washita at the commemoration in 1934, sixty-two years after the 1868 battle. Pallbearers are some of the most important men in the Cheyenne tribe. From L to R: Jacob Runner, Yellow Eyes, Chief Magpie, Philip White Shield, and John Otterby. Photo no. 368. Courtesy of Western History Collections, University of Oklahoma Libraries.

Part Two:

Family Histories

Chapter Three

ANNA OTTERBY HAWK FAMILY

Anna Otterby Hawk was born in the eastern part of the Cheyenne–Arapaho territory near Bridgeport, Oklahoma, about 1900. Her mother was Wolf Belly Woman, a full-blood Cheyenne who had survived the Sand Creek Massacre, and her father was John Otterby, the son of Chief White Hawk, a descendant of a French trapper on the Upper Missouri River, Fenancais Autobee. John's French grandfather, Charles Autobee, married Cheyenne Picking Bones Woman, so his father was one-half Cheyenne and one-half French-Canadian. John worked as an agency farmer for the territorial government and as a U.S. civil service interpreter for the Cheyenne and Arapaho.

Anna was the youngest of three girls. Her Cheyenne name, First Killer Woman, was given to her by her great-grandfather. He had been awarded the name in early days, for being the first person in his raiding party to kill an enemy. According to custom, the grandfather named the newborn child with the name of a deceased relative or someone with a "pretty name." Gradually the practice of the grandmother naming the first-born became more common. Cheyenne names, for the most part are gender-specific, and they usually come from the natural world. There are two different sets of names—one is for boys and another for girls. The boys' names tend to come from predatory birds or animals and war experiences, and girls' names are likely to be associated with the earth and more sedentary animals. Sometimes both sexes use names from the same list of possibilities, and sometimes people change their names. One example comes from Heap of Crows, who liked the name of the government agent, so he took the agent's name, Miles, and became John Miles. One very important aspect of the naming system is that it helps people keep track of who is related to whom, and who are possible marriage candidates since there is a prohibition on marrying any relative, no matter how distant the relationship.

A self-professed tomboy, Anna had her own horse. She and her friend liked to ride down by the creek and practice jumping upon their horses' backs. One time when she jumped, she missed and landed on the ground, a story she related that she thought was very funny. Her favorite activity, when awake, was to accompany her father on horseback as he traveled over the large Cheyenne–Arapaho Reservation area advising various Cheyennes on how to plant and care for vegetable gardens. The Cheyenne diet, being heavily weighted with meat and flour products, lacked important vitamins and minerals necessary for a balanced diet, so he stressed raising and eating vegetables. He also taught the Cheyenne how to raise crops they could sell in the market place, and he introduced to them the practice of castrating chickens to produce plumper, more tender meat.

Anna bemoaned the fact that she never had the opportunity to go to school and learn a skill. She knew that there was some connection between her lack of education and the cycle of poverty in which her family was now trapped. She also understood that her grandchildren could never break out of that cycle of poverty without a proper education. An education was essential for them to learn independence and be gainfully employed someday in the future. But chances of that happening to Cheyenne young persons in 1974 were very slim, especially in the rural areas of the state. Today their chances are much better.

In 1915, at the age of fifteen, Anna enrolled in the Red Moon School that she attended for two years. In 1917 she met her future husband, Amos White Hawk, the son of Chief White Hawk, at the annual Indian fair in nearby Elk City. Shortly thereafter, the couple married and settled on the banks of the Washita River as part of Chief White Shield's camp. In the next eighteen years she and Amos had seven children—three girls and four boys.

Amos White Hawk had some experience in electronics, but he always seemed to be traveling to find work. He was able to find temporary work at times, but could never seem to find anything permanent. He succumbed to alcohol at an early age in the late 1960s. Anna married a second time the Indian way, but the marriage did not last long.

Anna Hawk, age 74, Norman, Oklahoma. Author's photo. 1974.

In 1974, when I met Anna, she was a widow of seventy-four living in a house filled with family. Shortly before I arrived, one son, Hank, who was afflicted with cirrhosis, had left his three children and his wife in California so that he could come back to Hammon and die in his mother's home. The other three sons lived with her part or all of the year. All were divorced, one remarried, and each had three or four children. All were unemployed and without sources of income except for some monthly welfare checks. They, therefore, were unable to contribute any significant amount to household finances.

At this time in her life, Anna had a total of twenty-seven grandchildren and thirteen great-grandchildren. Three of the grandchildren and one son lived in her house on a fairly permanent basis, and all were totally dependent on her financially and emotionally. A second son, Freeman, was the father of three of the grandchildren: Ann, Junior, also called Freeman, and Teresa. All of them lived in Anna's house on a full-time basis. Freeman, the father, and his wife were in the process of getting a divorce, and the children were sent to grandmother's house.

The third son, Leslie, and his wife also had three children and two grandchildren. They went to Anna's (his mother's) house in Hammon five or six times a year for extended visits. Leslie derived much needed support from Anna. He was not employed. He had no training in any kind of specialty work that would qualify him for some jobs, but he was well liked by everyone as evidenced by having been elected twice to serve on the powerful tribal business committee for which he was paid a salary.

One day a television crew from Oklahoma City came to Hammon to film Anna and Martha Fingernail in Martha's house. Just as the filming began, Anna's youngest son, Mickey, came bursting in the door with a friend to tell his mother that her good, long-time friend, Lillie Hayes, had died and asked if he could have a note authorizing a charge of five dollars to Anna's account at the grocery store. In the shock of the moment a highly emotional response was anticipated by the son and his friend. So Anna quickly wrote a note, as he had requested. One hour later he returned and he said that it had all been a mistake. "Lillie Hayes has not died after all. It was just a rumor." It was something she should have known, and she was upset that she had let her son trick her. Based on prior experiences, she was certain that he had bought beer using her credit. In contrast to the sons, Anna's three daughters were fairly independent financially. All were married, had children, and lived in distant towns. Lorene, who had eight children and four grandchildren, lived in California, and Frances who lived in Clinton, Oklahoma, had three children and seven grandchildren.

Anna Hawk, on the right; and counter-clockwise, her sister, Minnie, unknown person, and three daughters: Frances, Lorene, and Beulah. Courtesy, Wanda Queenan.

Beulah, the daughter who lived in Oklahoma City, probably had the closest relationship with her mother. She and her husband, who was employed, had three sons. Although Beulah lived one hundred twenty miles away, she drove to her mother's home at least once a week, if not twice. She was an expert bead worker, and she sought her mother's advice on designs and skins. None of Beulah's three children attended school or worked at any kind of job, and she worried and fretted constantly about what would happen to them. When she visited her mother, she often brought one of them with her so that Anna could lecture the young person on, in Beulah's words, "gettin' an education or gettin' a job."

Anna's daughter Lorene, who lived in California, had a heart attack in 1974, and Anna sold some of her best moccasins to raise money for a bus ticket. She knew that Irene needed help with the grandchildren and great grandchildren, and especially after a heart attack. She loved her family and she always gave them first priority. She believed that just seeing a family member helped the person get better, and it seemed to do so.

The third daughter, Frances, who lived in nearby Clinton, had three grandchildren in her home, but she and Anna had disagreements, so there was very little contact between them.

John Otterby and his daughter, Anna Otterby Hawk. Photo no. 21062.2, Christopher C. Stoltz, Rev. James Noble Collection. Courtesy, Research Division of the Oklahoma Historical Society.

Traveling to the source of a family problem was always one of Anna's priorities. She had an old car that she described as "just a piece of junk," and it finally broke down for good. Then she had to find a ride with some relative or friend, and sometimes I would give her a ride. No matter how scarce money became, overseeing or helping with a distant relative's problem was more important to her than anything else, and family members expected her to come. By virtue of her caring personality, wisdom, and her economic resources, Anna was the most important decision maker in the family.

One day one of her teenage granddaughters, Elizabeth, and friend arrived from Albuquerque for a visit. Both were sixteen and in their own words, "just drifting," and they planned to stay awhile. I had stopped to pick up Anna to take her to Oklahoma City. When we got ready to leave, Anna turned to say to Elizabeth, "Don't get in my things while I'm gone." Elizabeth answered in an aside "as if I'm a child." Then Anna cautioned them to "Be good." I asked Anna how she was going to get back to Hammon and Elizabeth answered, "She'll find a way. She always finds a way."

Anna's small frame house that she had bought with her 1968 claim check from the Indian Claims Commission plus money from the sale of some inherited land was falling apart. She knew her house was "very poor." Her roof leaked for eight years before the Concho office repaired it, and she was quite certain that "the shingles on her roof are just tar paper, and the fixtures that Concho puts in the houses are the cheapest that they can buy."

An official from the Bureau of Indian Affairs announced in 1975 that since her house was beyond repair, it was not worth saving and recommended that she buy one of the new government Indian houses on the highway that were priced at $14,000. The new house would require only a forty-dollar payment per month for forty years. But she declined for several reasons: "The new Indian houses are dumps in a few years anyway. They are very poor, and they have no regular floors. And when I die, my sons might not make a payment, and then they would lose the whole house. Besides, I like my house even if it is a dump."

Anna's claim that "Cheyennes are used to livin' all crowded together" is probably accurate, but her added claim that "Indians like it, bein' all crowded in a tepee," is probably overstated. She acknowledged that there were definite advantages to a house over a tent, the most important being that a house was easier to heat in the winter. But as she pointed out, "It takes money to pay utilities in town. On the river, we could always find wood to build a fire."

What was frustrating for everyone in the Hammon Cheyenne community was that they had to depend on the Business Committee to decide the priority of their repairs—who got them and how much could be spent. The repairs did not keep up with the number of requests, the money needed was always in short supply, and the carpenters and plumbers hired were inexperienced, but it was the only way the Cheyenne could finally have a halfway livable house. It was a given that close relatives and "pets" of the tribal councilman were at the top of the repair list. It certainly did not help to be located a greater distance from tribal headquarters than everyone else as the Hammon Indians were.

Anna Hawk verbalized her frustration with the whole process, "For five years that man said he would fix my house. Five hundred forty dollars was allotted, and boys training to be carpenters and plumbers did the job. They did a sorry job, left holes in the floor, and when I pointed that out to that man, the housing manager, he just said that those were the boys that had to be used. I know that they did not use but maybe one hundred fifty of the five hundred forty dollars, and then they said there just was not any more money."

Anna's income was difficult to stretch for her family's necessities, especially for the utilities, which seemed to be the hardest to pay. In 1974 she received two checks monthly, an Old Age check for $137 and an AFDC check for $164. From those checks, added to any beadwork income, she had to pay for all household expenses. In the summers she had extra income from teaching missionaries the basics of how to learn a language of an indigenous group of people at the Language Institute in Norman, Oklahoma, but one dollar and twenty-five cents per hour did not add up to much.

Many Indian families needed food stamps, but how to obtain them was not fully understood by everyone. Anna liked to use food stamps when she could, because "they help a lot. I've been trying to save up so I can get some. I have to have thirty dollars. They say, 'Why don't you just take part of your check and use it to buy food stamps?' But it's hard. Nobody knows how hard it is for us Indians."

An added difficulty for all is that the nearest supermarket, which has lower food prices, is eighteen miles away. Most Cheyenne are forced by inadequate or no transportation to trade at the local grocery store that is within walking distance for everyone. At the small market in Hammon, food is more expensive, but groceries can be bought on credit, a privilege that is not available at the Elk City supermarket. One solution available to a few Cheyenne is to shop for groceries at the air base commissary in Altus, Oklahoma, which is about seventy-five miles away. There, the U.S. government allows active and retired military personnel and their immediate families to have commissary privileges. Savings allegedly amount to about ten to fifteen percent.

Scarcity of money was the primary reason that most families had insufficient and poor quality food. Some of the white population, being acutely aware of the dire need for food in the Indian community, out of empathy and a sense of charity, made available to Indians food resources that would be disposed of otherwise. The white rancher who notified local Indians that he had to dispose of a crippled or frozen cow was regarded as a true friend. After one of the Indian men butchered the animal, and one of the women sliced it and dried it, the meat could be preserved for future use.

Anna was an important person in her community. Others sought her advice, and she was constantly concerned about their welfare. At least three times in the past she served as the substitute midwife because the regular midwife was not available. In spite of her severe financial straits, Anna understood the importance of being able to help others. Near the end of the month, when food for the Indian community was always in short supply and welfare checks were not due until the first, Anna was often asked for money or food, and she always responded if she could. In her words, "Sunday, a woman came to my house and said, 'Anna, you got any flour? Or maybe some cornmeal?' You know, I always keep commodities, and then you can mix water with it to make food or somethin' to eat. Bein' poor is nothin' new for us Cheyennes. We were poor in the old days, and we're poor today. There's no difference, but the men were happy then. Today none of 'em are happy. They have no jobs, and they have nothin' to do. Nobody knows how hard it is for us Indians. And somebody has to help. And I help everybody."

Anna felt a special kinship with those who were poor. She liked to share with as many as she could because she knew what it was like to be poor. One of her favorite stories was about the time she was in New Mexico and had her shoes shined by a "poor little Mexican boy." She paid him and then gave him a tip, a dime. She wanted him and others standing nearby to know how generous she was, "I help everybody."

Her economic resources, although greater than those of anyone else in the family, were quite limited. But she always seemed to make the most of what she had. What discouraged her more than anything else was her feeling that the white man had left her with few options by which to survive. He was especially responsible for her being confined to a barren land. In her words: "I'm too old now. The soil is poor and it takes too much work to get anything to grow. There aren't any rabbits to catch and eat anymore because the white man poisoned them because they were gettin' in his crops."

Pastor Max Malone, of the Indian Baptist Church in Hammon, raised rabbits and occasionally brought one to her. Being exceedingly skilled at jerking meat, she sliced it into thin slices and dried it to be preserved, leaving nothing to be wasted.

In the spring of 1977, Anna walked to a friend's house and said: "Everybody in my family's sick. I can't help 'em anymore. I've got to find somebody to take care of the grandchildren cause I'm gonna' die."

Early one morning, three weeks later, Anna's two youngest grandchildren awakened to find their grandmother dead. Junior went to the pastor's house for help and came back home and told his sister they had to go to school because that was what his grandmother would have wanted.

As the family began to gather for the funeral, the personality and authority vacuum was obvious. Minor disputes broke out over who should get Anna's personal belongings. The two big decisions that had to be made were: What happens to the four grandchildren? Who gets the house? Several Indian families in the community offered to take the children. An aunt as well as their father wanted them, but the mother of the children, who had traveled a great distance, was preferred not only by the welfare worker, but the children. However, Junior wanted to come to my house. He did and it was a wonderful experience for all of us, but he got homesick to see his family, so he went to live with his mother in Minnesota.

One year after Anna's death, the disposition of the house had still not been settled and no one had gone to the Indian agency at Concho, Oklahoma, to initiate a legal property settlement. One daughter's comments seemed to reflect the feelings of the others, "I wonder what Mama wanted to do with the house."

Anna was the dominant family personality, and her death left a void that could not be easily filled. None of the sons or daughters felt capable of stepping forward to assume Anna's role. The self interest that each of them had suppressed while Anna was alive surfaced. Each attempt that a son or daughter made to impose his or her will on the others was met with anger. They refused to cooperate with each other. The order and cooperation that had kept the family functioning smoothly under Anna's direction shattered at her death.

Who would now assume Anna's role was dependent on many factors, but the two daughters who were in good health and had income from beadwork, welfare, or employment were probably the strongest contenders. Leadership potential, compassion for others, and commitment to Indian values of sharing and cooperation were crucial requirements for Anna's replacement. The special dependent relationship between Anna and the adult children that had been accepted as a way of life and nurtured and enjoyed by Anna for so many years enabled the family to be a cohesive functioning unit that could respond to any crisis. Now someone needed to replace her.

It has never been easy to change one's role of dependency to one of responsibility, but if enough demands are put on the family, one member must assume a leadership role or the family is likely to disintegrate.

No one surfaced to take Anna's role. Beulah, the most likely candidate, lost both legs to diabetes and died of kidney failure. All of

Anna's sons died prematurely, and in 1978, Lorene died of a heart attack. The death thirty years later of Anna's only remaining child, Frances, marked the last of the first and second generations of Anna's family. In 2007 none of her descendents were living in the Hammon area, but one granddaughter was living in Yukon, one of Oklahoma City's suburbs. Freeman, or Junior, her grandson, lives in Brown's Ferry, Minnesota.

Chapter Four

MARTHA SWALLOW
FINGERNAIL FAMILY

Martha Swallow Fingernail was a positive, happy woman who, at the age of sixty-four, headed a four generation family. She lived by a code of self-sacrifice and generosity. She was one of four children born to Cheyenne parents near Calumet, Oklahoma, in 1910. Her mother died shortly after her birth, and she and her three siblings were raised by her mother's sister. Not until Martha had a family of her own, many years later, did she learn that her aunt was not her biological mother.

At the age of fifteen, in 1925, she married Pete Fingernail, the son of Chunky Fingernail, who was the grandson of Chief White Shield and Fish Woman. Both Cheyenne, they were from the Hammon area. For the next twenty-five years, Martha and Pete lived in a tepee in the small camp of Chief White Shield on the Washita River and raised a family of five daughters—Nadine, Christine, Joyce, Louise, Tonita, and one son, Martin. Martha, by combining her tribal claim check of $2,300 with that of her husband and of her husband's brother, was able to buy a four-bedroom house for $6,900 and move her family from the camp down by the river into town. She felt very fortunate because the extra space had always been needed to accommodate the ten to fifteen people who slept at her house each night and the fifteen to twenty who ate in her kitchen.

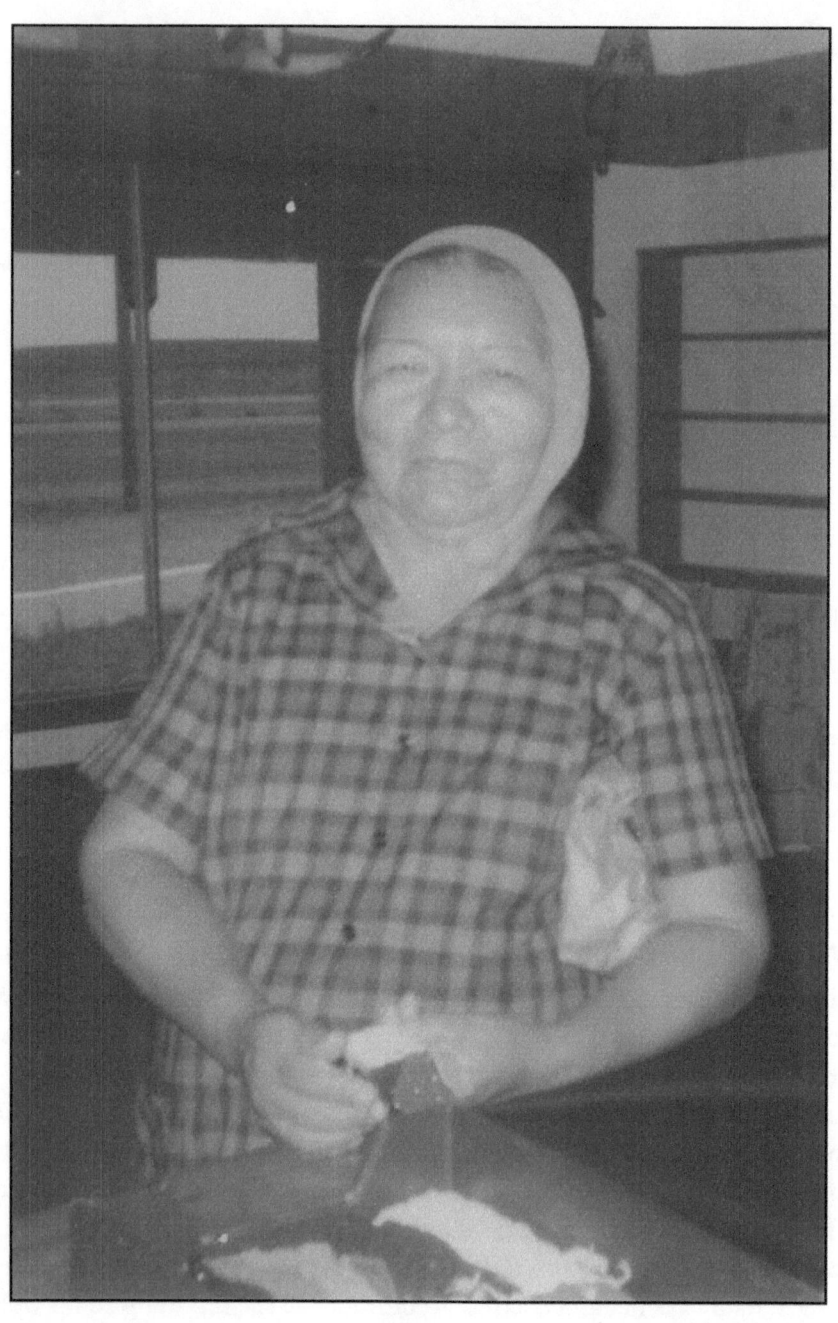

Martha Swallow Fingernail June 1971.Courtesy, Wanda Queenan.

Martha missed seeing her friends and family when she moved into town. She reminisced about the old days on the riverbank of the Washita River:

> Those were happy years. My husband sometimes had a job. You know he'd work for farmers at cattle-branding time, so there was money, though not very much. Some of the Indian men worked then. And some lost their money, but the alcohol was not as bad. With the move to town, there was trouble with alcohol, and the men can't get jobs today. Nobody will hire 'em. Whites don't like Indians, but in the old days they used to visit us down on the river. They helped us some. Now only the old ones help.

By the time the family moved into town, two of her daughters had already established their own households. The three remaining daughters, one son, five grandchildren, Martha's husband, and her husband's brother moved into Martha's house. It was relatively large compared to others in Hammon, but the Fingernail family was a large group of twelve people.

Built in 1914, the house was in constant need of repair. Since Hammon was the most distant town from the Bureau of Indian Affairs headquarters in Concho, its houses were last on the repair list. The Cheyenne who made up the Business Committee, employed by the Bureau of Indian Affairs, selected the houses that they believed were in the greatest need of repair. They decided when the repair would occur and how much could be spent. Tribal members in Hammon understood that it always helped to have a friend or relative in Concho with some influence where the committees met. They complained constantly about the favoritism.

Martha had to wait two years for her leaky roof and broken plumbing to be repaired. Her greatest problem with the house was its inadequate heat in the winter. The two upstairs bedrooms were virtually unusable in the cold winter months, necessitating a sleeping arrangement of mattresses circling the small living room furnace from the middle of November to the middle of February.

Martha was a very pleasant person, and the main joys in her life were her grandchildren. She always had a smile. She waited on everyone to her own detriment. She was meticulous about keeping records. She had an antique book with brittle pages on which past family members had recorded tribal and family events dating from 1832 up to the present, and she kept it current. Births, marriages, and deaths were listed as well as major battles that were fought. Respected by the family, this book was considered a reliable reference for details of family and Cheyenne tribal events.

Pete, Martha's husband, was a very quiet man who had little to say. One day when I visited, he was in the back yard of the house butchering a cow from a white neighbor's ranch. The cow had fallen and broken its leg. When Pete and another Cheyenne finished the butchering, Martha sliced it into thin strips and hung it on the clothesline to dry. "This particular cow," said Pete "would furnish ample meat that would last through the winter and into next spring for all of the family."

The death of Pete, in 1975 at the age of seventy, and of his brother, Bert, also in 1975, left Martha's house without an adult male on a permanent basis. She felt fortunate, however, because she had a husband longer than almost any other Indian woman in the community.

Pete and Martha were enthusiastic youth workers while their children were growing up. They sponsored youth intertribal dances and Pete made the costumes. His brother, Bert, led the singers. Pete also organized baseball teams and had an enthusiastic following. Lawrence Hart reflected on the tireless leadership of the Fingernails: "I am grateful for this wholesome entertainment provided for me at an important time in my youth."

Pete's and Bert's deaths greatly increased Martha's economic burden. In 1978, she had one daughter (sometimes two), one son, seven grandchildren, and one great-grandchild living in her house. All monthly household expenses had to be paid out of her Old Age Pension check of $176 and AFDC (Aid to Families with Dependent Children) check of $136, which she received for two grandchildren, plus her daughter's welfare check. When she got her husband's annual lease money her

Old Age pension check was stopped for two months and so the money shortage continued.

Of Martha's four daughters also living in Hammon in 1975, Christine was the only one who was married, and her husband was one of the few Indian men in the community who was employed. His salary and his wife's beadwork supported their seven children. Scarce as money was in Martha's house, it was scarcer in her daughters' families. Martha helped out by keeping some of the grandchildren in her home and feeding others on a regular basis.

The widowed daughter was having great difficulty supporting her nine children and one grandson with a welfare check and beadwork, so Martha helped a great deal by assuming partial care of several of her children. Only her grandson, Bruce, whose mother was Nadine, lived in Martha's home on a permanent basis. His mother dropped in for brief visits periodically, but Martha nurtured him and assumed the primary responsibility for meeting his many needs. Other relatives who lived in the house temporarily and some who dropped by during the day might play with him or feed him, but Martha acted in the capacity of his primary care giver. When he grew up he enlisted in the army and went immediately to Korea. When he returned, he moved back with his mother, but he came by to see his grandmother every morning before he went to work and most afternoons. At the age of twenty-nine he met an early death from internal injuries sustained during a fight with other Cheyennes. The deaths of Bert, Pete, and Bruce in a period of three years left Martha with a painful void. Losing a husband was something she was prepared for, but not a grandson who was someone special and who had his whole life ahead of him. She had been very attached to him and he to her.

Although every bed and mattress in her house was occupied most of the time, other relatives came to visit for extended periods. Being crowded did not deter visitors because they knew there was always room for one more pallet on the floor. Grandchildren in their late teens and twenties were the most frequent temporary visitors.

Martha related how county authorities appeared at her house one day without warning and took away her three grandchildren, ages two, five, and six, whom she was caring for. The authorities told her they were putting the children in a foster home for a few months, only until the "parents got straightened out." The parents were married, but separated, and the mother of the children had placed them with Martha, her mother, but that fact held no weight in the matter.

Six years later no one in the Hammon area had seen or heard anything about the children—where they were, how they were being treated, if they were being raised like a Cheyenne or like a white child. Martha Fingernail, the grandmother, with tears in her eyes, communicated their feelings of helplessness:

> We tried and tried to find out where they were but we couldn't.
> Me and my daughter went over there and talked to the judge,
> and he cussed us out. We tried to find out if they're adopted
> out, but we couldn't find out nothin'. I know he wouldn't do
> that to white people. We never found out where they were—
> for six years. One day a friend saw the youngest boy in a nearby
> town, just walkin' down the street. Some others saw him in
> somebody's front yard, but we couldn't find out nothin.' It
> takes money to find out things like that, and we don't have any
> money.

When Pete died in 1975, Joyce and her four children moved to Martha's house and stayed there until 1977. Joyce had a very close relationship with her mother, and she hoped that by moving there she could help alleviate some of the feelings of grief and loneliness that both she and her mother were experiencing. She rented the house in which she had been living in order to have some extra income, but unfortunately shortly after the rental family moved in, the mother of the family renters died there, which meant that according to custom the house had to be vacated and left empty for a period of several years. It was considered dangerous to be near the dead or anything or any place that the dead had associated with because the Cheyenne believed that the dead were contaminated and that their ghosts hovered about ready to cause evil happenings. After three months, however, the daughter decided to defy custom and re-rent the house because she could no longer afford to do without the rent money.

Joyce worked when she could find employment, but jobs were limited in Hammon. Although she found several jobs in neighboring Elk City, she was never able to get to them regularly because her car kept breaking down, and there was no other transportation available for her.

Martha was particularly distressed because the two grandsons assumed no responsibility for themselves or the family. They attended school sporadically and could sometimes be found sleeping on her living room floor until noon. Not only did the boys not contribute to the household finances, they also did not help with household chores or responsibilities. Martha lamented, "I know I need the weather stripping for my door, but if I had it, nobody would put it up. The boys never do anything. It's hard when there isn't a man because there's no one to fix things. There's nobody but me."

When another daughter, who was divorced, remarried, she brought two children from her first marriage to Martha's house so that Martha could take care of them. and Martha became a surrogate mother. The four children from the daughter's second marriage lived with their biological parents. Martha liked this son-in-law very much because he was "a good man—a good worker." He operated a bulldozer and worked on farms and construction projects. Martha was always delighted when he and her daughter came to visit: "She is the only daughter, except Christine, who works when she comes home. No one around here ever helps. There are twelve of us, and I cook, I sweep, I wash, and nobody else does anything. I say to them, 'What will you do if I die? You won't be able to do anything.'"

A real test came for the family when Martha, who was diabetic, suffered a nerve paralysis on the right side of her face and was hospitalized for one week. The cooking was managed by members of the family as they became hungry, but other household tasks were left undone. The daughters who lived nearby sent an older child or two to help out with the care of the children, but things did not run smoothly. One daughter remarked: "We didn't know what to do. We kept goin' over to see Mama

49

at the hospital. We couldn't tell she was gettin' any better, and she kept worryin' about the children."

When Martha came home from the hospital, another brother, from Wyoming, came to take her to see two Indian medicine men in Wyoming who he thought could help her. But Martha never got to go because her brother's granddaughter was killed suddenly in a car accident, and he had to return to Wyoming without Martha.

Martha's recovery was very gradual, and although she still could not move about very easily, she had full responsibility for the household again. Difficult tasks, such as hanging the laundry outside in the below-freezing temperatures, were usually assumed by someone else in the family, but the permanence of this help became very erratic as Martha continued to improve. When she felt somewhat better, one month later, she traveled to Denver to visit another brother, who was terminally ill with cancer. Two daughters from Hammon and the son, who happened to be at his mother's house on an extended visit, were left to run Martha's household. This time there was open dissension about who had final authority. Joyce, the only one who had a job, was buying groceries for the entire family. Her siblings would not accept any responsibility and questioned Joyce's demands that they do so. They accused her of trying to take over just because she was a permanent resident in their mother's house, getting free rent, and felt that she had no right to tell them what to do.

Competition, jealousy, and arguments among the siblings came very close to causing a complete breakdown of the functioning of the extended family when Martha was unable, for reasons of illness or absence, to function as the family head. To complicate matters further, the conditions for the renewal of a new land lease from which Martha and her children received some yearly income could not be agreed upon by Martha's children. One wanted a five-year lease while the others wanted a shorter lease in case land prices went up. The farmer who had been leasing the land finally declared that he was tired of all the bickering, and he would just find some other land. The consequence was no lease and no money for anyone.

One daughter commented, "If Mama'd been here, it never would have happened." Although all members of the family may not have agreed with Martha, in the final analysis Martha had their respect and they abided by her decisions because they knew she loved all of them and had no other interests but theirs. Their world, which depended so much on the Indian values of sharing, had held together very well as long as she directed it. Martha did not have much faith in the next generation, but, she said, "I close my eyes and pray that somebody will know what to do when I die." Ten years later Martha went to a church meeting at her daughter's house and, according to Tonita, "She came back home, and sat down in a chair, and just fell over. It was a heart attack." At her death in 1987 Martha was seventy-seven.

In 2006, of Martha's six children, two were deceased. Martin had died in the seventies of cirrhosis, and Nadine had died from complications of diabetes. Christine, Louise, Joyce, and Tonita were still living in Hammon, each in a separate house with one or more of their children or grandchildren, and Joyce was teaching Cheyenne at the local high school. Unfortunately in the Fingernail family every sibling and many of their children had diabetes, some in a more virulent form than others.

Lillie Anna Elk River Hayes, her husband, Darwin Hayes, and daughters, Cootsie and Marietta, Photo no. 710 c. 1917. Darwin Hayes Collection Courtesy, Research Division of the Oklahoma Historical Society.

Chapter Five

LILLIE ELK RIVER HAYES FAMILY

Lillie Elk River Hayes, grandmother and great-grandmother, was a remarkable woman. She, at age eighty-eight in 1974, was one of the oldest and most respected Cheyenne in Hammon. Fairly active and alert, she was a very prolific bead worker who had learned the craft at age ten. In her words: "I don't know how many moccasins I have made, but many, many. I made many buckskin dresses, as many as four for one daughter, many fully-beaded cradle boards, but only one beaded bedspread, all from buckskin. And I have made seven big tepees—my last one two years ago for my son. Only certain Indian women were designated to make tepees and mine were made from canvas, and beaded in original designs" (*ECDN*: December 12, 1971).

Although failing eyesight in her later years diminished her production considerably, she continued to bead every day. She spoke only the Cheyenne language, which became somewhat of a disadvantage as other Cheyenne speakers of her generation were dying. She could communicate with her friends and her children in Cheyenne, but she needed an interpreter to communicate with most of her grandchildren and great-grandchildren, all of whom spoke only English.

Lillie Elk River Hayes, the daughter of Chief Elk River (the person for whom Elk City was named), was born in 1884 in the Hammon area when it was the part of the Cheyenne-Arapaho Reservation. Lillie grew up in a traditional Cheyenne family and lived on the banks of the

Washita River the greater part of her life. She married Darwin Hayes in 1906 when she was twenty-two, and they had two daughters, Cootsie Hayes Littleman, Marietta Hayes Orange, and one son, Gus Hayes.

When Cootsie was about eight, in 1917, Lillie, Darwin, and their three children moved to Hammon from the Clinton area, so they could enroll Cootsie in the third grade at Red Moon School. Cootsie remembered that she liked school except for the school policy that did not allow any student to speak a single Cheyenne word. One day she fell and injured her hip. She was taken to an Elk City doctor who opted to do nothing, a decision that doomed her to have a pronounced limp for the rest of her life. Cootsie hazily recalled: "I guess that the doctors didn't know very much. They didn't know what to do. Now they can't fix my leg because it's been too long. "I didn't go back to the Red Moon School, not after I hurt my leg, but three years later I went to the Hammon Public School."

Ten years later Cootsie had grown up and married. She had one son, Leroy, and three daughters, Irene, Nellie Mae, and Margaret. In a short time her first marriage had ended, and Cootsie then met Louis Littleman, a Cheyenne who had just been discharged from military service in World War II. A committed military man, Louis believed that his military service had been the best period of his life. Simply thinking about the excitement of being a soldier and fighting against Italians and Germans in Africa kept him occupied for hours at a time. He reminisced about the thrills of battle and declared, "What I really want to be is a warrior. That was as close as I'll ever get."

When the war was over, Louis came back home only to find that everybody and everything had changed. The worst was that his wife had left him. He deeded his farm to his son, and the son left for California to teach flying. The son never returned or communicated again with his father.

Louis's early years had been difficult ones. Most of what he remembered of his early and later life was the unpleasant, unfair, and degrading treatment by whites.

Louis had had a hard life. He lost his mother at the age of four. His father remarried, and he, his brother, and his sister were expected to assume considerable responsibility at an early age. Every day he milked the cows, harnessed the horses, and performed numerous other chores necessary to eke a living out of the small family farm.

When he turned sixteen, his family decided that he should go away to school to get a good education. The agency sent him to the Carlisle Indian School in Pennsylvania, the first off-reservation school for Indians in the United States, and his father's half-sister agreed to pay his extra expenses. Six months later, World War I broke out, and Carlisle School became a military post. Louis returned home and finished his secondary education at the Chilocco Indian School in Indian Territory.

After his military service, Louis and Cootsie were married, and they moved into a tepee near Cootsie's parents on the banks of the Washita River where they remained until 1951 when Lillie's husband, Darwin Hayes, died. Cootsie and her mother, Lillie, moved into the town of Hammon with the two children, Dorothy and William. Louis decided to remain in the river camp and live by himself which he did for a long time, a period that he estimated to be "about two or three years."

Louis tried farming again, but after twelve years of struggling, he quit. He explained, "I got the lazy bug. I had cattle, horses. Sometimes we could make thirty or forty dollars a week from cream. We had a few hogs. We had eggs. But they got so cheap nobody would buy them. Sometimes we only got ten cents a dozen. Well, I got the lazy bug. Yeah, the lazy bug has hit everybody. Now there is modern farm equipment. Everybody had to have money to farm and change his ways. It was just too hard."

Louis was always on center stage. He had a well-developed sense of humor that served him well as a storyteller. He especially liked to tell stories about the white man. He recalled with disgust, almost anger, an experience he had with some white travelers when he was a gasoline station attendant at the nearby Cherokee Trading Post. The gas station and curio shop were located on Highway 66 that has since been upgraded to Interstate-40. In Louis's words:

> People from the east over there by the ocean would come in there and not believe that they were seein' a real Indian. That's that new buildin' over there by the new highway. It was a big curio shop. We were supposed to be sellin' Indian things. Mostly it was sellin' Hong Kong. Those people from the east—they didn't know the difference. I put on my war bonnet and would charge one dollar for a picture. One day I made sixteen dollars. One day a family came in there, and they were eyein' me from top to bottom. They said, "Where did you learn to speak American?" I said, "My language is American. Yours is English. I learned to speak your language way back when I was a papoose. There was a battle and I was left all alone. The white man came and took me to live with him. I learned to speak English." And do you know? They believed it. Those people just acted crazy. They kept wantin' to know if I was real.

Louis finally got disgusted with his job and quit. "I never worked again," he proudly announced. Louis was very proud of his Cheyenne heritage. He was particularly proud to be the keeper of the ceremonial pipe for the tribe's Arrow Ceremony, and of being the grandson of an earlier Keeper of the Sacred Arrows, an honor reserved for a very respected man in the tribe. He also had served as a priest in the Native American Church. But the sense of importance that he derived from his tribal position and the popularity he enjoyed for his much sought-after-advice clearly did not spill over into his domestic life.

In 1974, after Louis and Cootsie had been married for thirty years, Louis announced, "We fight like cats and dogs." Cootsie reiterated, "Yeah, we fight like cats and dogs, but that's because Louis will never grow up. He's wrong all the time." Daily life was like an ongoing contest to see who got the last word. Irene, Cootsie's daughter, said that in spite of what they said, they couldn't live without each other. On the surface they appeared to have a fairly egalitarian relationship, but in actuality, Cootsie won more arguments than Louis. In financial matters, she made all of the decisions. That was true even when Louis was the sole recipient of income in the house. He could not qualify for Social Security but he got an Old Age Pension instead, the same one that she would also get when she turned sixty-five. She and Louis lived on Louis's Old Age Pension of $154 and a veteran's check of $17 each month. Her only other income was $23 each year from the leasing of land from an allotment that she shared with thirty-nine other people. She never had income from beading because she found it too difficult.

One reason Cootsie made all of the financial decisions was that Louis was not interested in small-scale budgeting and in trying to budget an inadequate amount of money. If there was not enough money at the end of the month, then it was not his fault, he argued. Besides, Cootsie was more skilled at getting credit extended at the grocery store than he was. She always tried to pay off part of their two hundred dollar bill on the first, so she could charge at the end of the month. The charge account was their safety cushion.

In the 1970s Louis and Cootsie moved to one of the U.S. government houses located on Highway 34 that was already in dire need of repair. But Cootsie understood they were lucky to have a house with real brick siding because some of the government houses had plastic brick that was cracking. Louis blamed Cootsie because she bought it without his knowledge. But she dismissed the charge saying, "I'm used to him complainin."

The greatest sources of arguments and hard feelings between them were the divorce settlement of Louis's first marriage and his life insurance policy of ten thousand dollars. Louis kept reminding Cootsie that someday she would get a lot of money. When he had an emergency appendectomy, he accused her of wanting him to die because of the money. She explained why she was so upset, "I only get it if he dies. I don't get anything else. His children don't get anything else. He made a deed transferring his land to the son of his first wife if he died first. I keep telling him to go change it before he dies so his other children would get something, but he never goes."

Cootsie decided to punish him for not changing his will by refusing to see him in the hospital. Some family members believed that her neglect of him contributed heavily to his much prolonged hospital stay, one that lasted many months. The sicker he became, the more adamant she became about not seeing him, and the more the community talked about it. But Cootsie remembered that one time when she was sick she went to the doctor in Clinton. She recalled, "I had a terrible headache. The doctor gave me three shots. I was kinda crazy, and Louis came in and said, 'Just go ahead and die. Go ahead. Die. I don't care.' I'm not gonna hold his hand. He's just a big baby. He wants everybody to feel sorry for him."

Louis really believed that he could not get well. Six months earlier, he had made a vow that his stepson, Leroy, would be the next pipe keeper in the Arrow Ceremony and, as a friend explained, "The son started goin' to a church down in Elk City and by May," according to one Indian man, "he was dropped by this preacher. He found that he wasn't welcome. As a consequence, he didn't go to the Arrow Ceremony. Louis was embarrassed and upset because if a Cheyenne vow isn't kept then somethin' bad will happen. Louis feels he can't get well. He's just given up."

Louis never knew anything but disappointment from his son and stepson. He deeded a farm to his oldest son who left for California and never returned. Louis spoke of it with great sadness. His stepson, who was Cootsie's son, was not welcome in the house because he had difficulty controlling his consumption of alcohol. Cootsie elaborated, "He even beat up on his grandmother, Lillie. He got a skillet and hit her on the head. But she's still the only one who really loves him. I tell him if his grandmother dies, that no one will take care of him. No one will live with that but his grandmother."

Cootsie's daughter, Irene, was also very tolerant of her brother's behavior. She never showed anger when he took money or food from her house, and she assumed responsibility for posting bond for him when and if needed. She fully understood that he was ill and needed help.

Irene and her second husband, who was half-Kiowa and half-Cheyenne, made a special trip to Montana to take Louis for the annual Sun Dance and Arrow ceremonies. While there, Louis visited his daughter and her husband, a Pentecostal Holiness minister. Louis had a wonderful time because he ate fresh deer meat every day, and he was convinced that was why he felt better in Montana than he usually did at home. Upon their return, Irene and her husband discovered that their house had been rented to another family, so they moved in with her grandmother, Lillie Elk River Hayes.

Kathryn and Fred Hoffman. Elk City Powwow 1976. He is the son of Vinnie and Albert Hoffman, and she is the daughter of John Tyler Young Bull. Courtesy, Wanda Queenan.

In 1976 Lillie lived in the home that she owned. She had monthly income from her Old Age Pension, annual lease income from her land, and irregular income from beadwork. There was, relatively speaking, a great deal of abundance at her house, that fostered the clustering of many relatives there year round. Some stayed for a brief time, maybe only a few days, but others lived there for months at a time, a happening most likely to occur when food and money were in short supply in the visitors' homes. Lillie actually raised Leroy and Irene, two grandchildren who were Cootsie's son and daughter. They moved into Lillie's house for an extended period of time. Both were in their forties, divorced, and unemployed.

At the urging of the BIA, Lillie made out a will leaving all of her possessions to Leroy, her grandson. Relatives who were left out of the will were upset. According to Anna Hawk, a few of them in anger allegedly took advantage of her weakened physical condition by taking some of her checks and letting her have no money at all. Her situation became so intolerable for her that she offered her land to at least two other women in the community if they would agree to let her move in with them. One of the women was Anna Hawk, who declined.

Events took a different direction, however, when the granddaughter, Irene, moved into Lillie's home. She would not permit the other members of the family to abuse her grandmother. Although in the past she had been oblivious to some family problems, she, more than anyone else, began to show concern for her grandmother. She cared for the needs of other family members as well and effectively carried out the old Indian precept, "We Indians always help each other out."

With the passing years, she exhibited more of her grandmother's personal qualities that helped hold the family together—compassion, lack of selfishness, and resourcefulness. As her grandmother's position of authority decreased with advancing age, due mainly to physical weakness, Irene assumed increasing responsibilities, and she became the primary decision-maker in the family

In 1978 Leroy was killed in a car accident, and one month later his brother, Gus, had a fatal stroke. Lillie revisited her will and made the decision to leave her entire estate to Irene because Irene seemed to be the only person in the family assuming responsibility for other family members, and she was sharing as her grandmother had.

Many grandchildren were fostered through the years in Lillie's home because they were welcome, and Cootsie, who was Lillie's daughter, was not as receptive as her mother had been, but she did move Nellie Ann, daughter, and granddaughter, representing the third and fourth generations, into her and Louis's home after Nellie Ann was seriously injured in a car accident.

Louis became chronically ill after an appendectomy in 1975. He was so grateful that he had his stepdaughter close by because he believed that she was the only one in the family he could trust. Not only did Irene make certain that the doctors and nurses take proper care of her stepfather, but she served importantly as mediator in the arguments between him and her mother. Louis told her repeatedly, "When I die, you've gotta take care of everything." Her response, "Don't I always?"

But Louis did not die, at least not for five years, and he never completely recovered. Cootsie hardly visited him in the hospital even though he had four additional operations and spent at least two of the next four years in a hospital. Cootsie's frequently heard comment was, "You mean he's not gonna' die?"

After Louis's last hospitalization, he returned home in a weakened condition with a walker. Cootsie was too busy to help him, because she was helping her daughter, Nellie Ann, who had just moved into Cootsie and Louis's house. Louis was finally moved to a nursing home while waiting for space at the Veteran's Hospital. He was hopeful that physical therapy would enable him to regain use of his legs, but he never got strong enough to use his legs again without some kind of support.

Louis never found his economic niche in life. Although he was greatly respected by other members of the Indian community, only his stepdaughter, Irene, out of the many members of his family, loved and respected him. She was the only one who would travel seventy miles several times a week to visit him in the hospital.

Louis, always proud to be Cheyenne, was nevertheless aware that it was a disadvantage in this world. He showed me a newspaper article about the mysterious death of a local Cheyenne man in a Denver jail. The headline read, "Deputy heard saying, 'I hate Indians anyway.'" The story was about the sound of a blow having been heard after the comment, and the subsequent discovery of the dead Indian. Louis said as he shook his head, "I hear or read somebody say that almost everyday, 'I hate Indians anyway.'"

Lillie Elk River Hayes died in 1979 at the age of ninety-five. Louis died in 1980 and Cootsie in 1984.

In 2007 Irene was living in one of the government houses on the highway that divides Roger Mills and Custer counties. After her grandmother's death, she inherited her grandmother's house, and she moved into it with her second husband. After a remodeling job on the house was paid for and not delivered, her contentious marriage ended in divorce. Irene then sold her grandmother's house and moved to the house on the highway where she lives today with her son, Harvey Miles. She has worked until quite recently at the nursing home in Elk City, but she has too many back problems to continue. Because of her efforts to reach out to help solve her family's problems, her family is surviving. Her son, who is forty-five, has been instrumental in trying to set up a program for teenagers to keep them occupied with wholesome activities or some kind of community work in the summers and after school.

Chapter Six

VINNIE WHITE EAGLE HOFFMAN FAMILY

Fred Hoffman, an only child, was born in 1915 in Chief White Shield's camp on the Washita River. His mother, Vinnie White Eagle, was a full-blood Cheyenne and granddaughter of Chief White Shield. His father, Albert Hoffman, was half Cheyenne and half German, a fact that in later years would prompt Fred's comment, "I'm not a full-blood Cheyenne. I'm a quarter German and sometimes I hate to say it, but I'm ashamed of my white blood."

In 1918 when Fred was only three years old, Vinnie and Albert moved the family from the Cheyenne camp on the Washita River to Vinnie's assigned allotment that was approximately ten miles west of Hammon. The government built a permanent house and barn for her family, and the Hoffmans became the first and the only Cheyenne family in the Hammon area to make a permanent home on an allotment. After moving to the allotment, Albert attempted to farm for a brief period but finally abandoned his efforts after he had major surgery. To get through periods of scarcity, he worked for a white rancher who lived nearby. From that time forward the land was always leased to white farmers with the exception of five acres that the family retained for its own use.

The land that Vinnie inherited from her father, mother, and sister gave her the distinction of being the owner of the largest amount of land and mineral rights in the area, and consequently the recipient of an income comparatively larger than that of the majority of Cheyennes. But the income was never enough to cover the needs of the immediate family and emergency needs of relatives and friends. The reason that the income was inadequate at times was not because of the needs of the immediate family, but because Vinnie was a generous person who shared all she had with relatives and friends. She was especially amenable to helping favorite relatives, no matter how distantly related, especially anyone who wanted to enroll in vocational school or participate in any kind of educational program. She believed that education was one of the most worthwhile investments she could make, and several times she initiated financial support without being asked. Even though the money was sometimes "loaned," she never really expected to be paid back. When a nephew actually paid back all he had borrowed, she was both surprised and gratified.

Fred Hoffman's family sent him to a nearby rural school where most of the other students were white. The Hoffmans thought that white association was a definite advantage, but Fred experienced so much prejudice that he wanted to attend an Indian school. With a great deal of reluctance his parents finally agreed to let him go to Chilocco, the Indian boarding school located north of Newkirk, in today's north central Oklahoma.

Fred met pretty Kathryn Young Bull at a fair when she borrowed his skates. Shortly after that she and her mother moved to Hammon where she enrolled in the Red Moon School. She attended Red Moon for one year and then again met Fred. Kathryn, who was one-half Cheyenne, Sioux, and French and one-half Arapaho, also attended a boarding school, the Haskell Indian Institute in Kansas. Kathryn and Fred both recalled quite vividly how they were punished for speaking Cheyenne instead of English at their respective schools. Throughout Fred's life he would cite this as just one more bit of evidence that "the white man wants to do away with the Indian people."

Before a year had passed after they first met, she and Fred had married. Fred moved his new wife into his parents' lodge. His mother,

Vinnie, developed a great deal of admiration for her new daughter-in-law, and would state proudly, fifty years later, "I never had to get after her."

The first twenty-five years of marriage were very difficult for Kathryn. She gave birth to their eight children, and Fred gave her little help in raising them. He was sporadically employed at different jobs, some of which were in the Hammon area, but many were as far away as New Mexico. Kathryn seldom traveled with her husband because the jobs were usually temporary, and the moving of small children was extremely difficult. She stayed with her in-laws and got considerable help from them, financial as well as emotional.

Family finances seldom reached a critical stage for Kathryn's family because of her mother-in-law's income, Fred's intermittent contributions, and a large, five acre family garden.

When the depression hit in the 1930s, employment was not available to either Indian or white persons, and the government, to alleviate the extreme deprivation, issued food staples on a regular basis. Even this Indian family who had taken great pride in having adequate and dependable income from leasing and employment discovered that their security meant little in a depression when a white farmer could not pay his lease and an employer could not pay his workers.

During one of the severe winters, when the Hoffman family food supplies had dwindled to almost nothing, Vinnie Hoffman, the senior mother of the three-generation family, remained adamant about not accepting any charity. Fred recalled proudly that it was his wife, Kathryn, who solved the crisis. She was the mother of two small children, and she could not let her family starve. She was the only one in the family who was willing to swallow her pride and ask neighbors for food. On a cold, blustery day, she walked three miles to the nearest house belonging to the Cowherds, a white family, and asked for help. The family gave her a generous amount of what they had, and for the remainder of the winter, shared their food supply with the Hoffman family.

Kathryn had always believed that education and the ability to get along with whites were important for her children. During their childhood and youth she worked diligently to inculcate the importance of independence, education, and hard work into her children's thinking. She had considerable reinforcement from her in-laws, her mother-in-law in particular. She was also cognizant of the fact that other Indians in the community would not approve.

She remembered the isolation her children experienced at the school: "Our children didn't feel a part of the Indians in town. Our children were scorned at Hammon High School. Most of their friends were white. Everybody is always askin' me why my children are different. I just watched over 'em when they were growin' up. All of 'em graduated from high school, except one. And most of 'em had wanted to get an education so they could do somethin' to help their people. But our children have always been that way."

Kathryn believed that, with the help of Vinnie, she had been successful raising her children because five of her eight children had become fairly independent. The strong, dependent relationship of children and grandchildren with the most senior woman, which was characteristic of many Cheyenne families in Hammon, was somewhat weaker in Vinnie Hoffman's family. Part of the explanation was that Vinnie in 1975 was eighty-eight and her small frame had become somewhat fragile. At the same time, all the children retained strong ties with their parents as well as with their grandmother. They visited frequently, and they were confident enough to know that if they needed money or help with child-care responsibilities, they could expect a generous response. The success of each child can be attributed in part to his or her identification with values leading to success instilled by Kathryn and Vinnie, but the change that occurred in Fred's life made the greatest impact.

That change occurred when the youngest child was five, and the oldest child had already dropped out of high school. Fred made the decision to stop his heavy drinking and adopt the precepts of the Native American Church. Fred, speaking with great pride of the change in his life at age forty-five, said proudly, "I used to drink a lot. One day, I said, 'I'm an important man. Everybody respects me. I'm gonna' do somethin' for the Indian people.' That's when I started goin' to the Native American Church and I changed my life."

Fred then began to focus his energies in two different directions. First, he became involved in a number of tribal programs, in particular, education and health. He explained his epiphany, "One day I went to this meetin' and this man was sayin' 'the reason the Indian had so many problems was that he wasn't used to takin' care of himself. The Indian was just like a child. He acted like a child, and he was treated like a child. And the only way to make things better was with education.' I started thinkin' about that and I said, 'What we need is a scholarship program,' so I started one."

Second, Fred began to work actively for the legalization and distribution of peyote for use in the Native American Church. He became its president and traveled extensively to talk about and explain the physical and spiritual healing characteristics of peyote.

The most important outcome of Fred's intensive involvement in the Native American Church was the positive effect it had on his eldest son whose short-term employment pattern had been dictated by his drinking habits. Like his father, Archie joined the Native American Church and quit drinking. The most important aspect of his rehabilitation was that it changed his unemployable status to employable, and provided great relief to a family who had five children to support.

Vinnie, although partially blind, was a very self-sufficient woman of eighty-eight. She lived in a small house next to Fred and Kathryn's house. Whenever possible, she took care of the great-grandchildren who were frequent, long-term visitors in her home. When needed she usually got some help from her daughter or one of the grandchildren. Although she was partially blind, she never had a vision problem because one grandchild was always living with her or visiting on a long-term basis.

When Albert died, Archie, Kathryn and Fred's oldest son, and his wife quit their jobs at Concho and with two of their five children moved back to Hammon and into Vinnie's house. They divided their semi-permanent stay between Vinnie's house where they slept and Fred and Kathryn's house where they ate.

The second oldest son, Fred, stayed with Vinnie sporadically. A draftsman, he quit his job with a large corporation because he did not want to be transferred to the Middle East. He decided to come back home and stay with his grandmother for awhile. He was divorced from his wife, who lived with their two children in California. His parents expressed concern over the fact that he was the only one of their children who had not been baptized in the Mennonite Church.

Two of Katherine and Fred's daughters each left a child in Kathryn's care for brief to long periods of time so that they could be employed. The youngest daughter, Arlene, who at twenty was divorced from her one-half Comanche, one-half Mescalero Apache husband had difficulty keeping a job because she suffered from severe anemia and had to be hospitalized periodically. According to the doctors, her anemia was the main cause of her two miscarriages and one premature birth. Kathryn said she felt like the child's mother. Arlene went to Sayre Junior College in Sayre, Oklahoma, a nearby town, but left because of the prejudice she experienced. She then enrolled in Oscar Rose College in Del City, Oklahoma, where she took courses in medical technology.

Ida, Arlene's sister, began staying with Kathryn after the birth of her baby. She was divorced from her husband, who was an artist. When only a few months old, Ida's baby was placed in Kathryn's care, so that the child's mother could return to her job at the Committee of Concerns, a tribal agency in nearby Clinton, Oklahoma.

Two other daughters, Lucy and Thelma, were married, employed, and living in another area of the state. Although they were both fairly independent, they visited their parents frequently. Their husbands planted gardens in Hammon on the Hoffman plot of land, and in the summer the daughters and husbands came back weekly to check on the progress of the gardens.

❧

Tyler, Fred and Kathryn's youngest son, was an accountant, and he was living with his Laguna Pueblo wife and child in Albuquerque, New Mexico. He had previously worked in Concho for IAT.

Fred and Kathryn had a fairly egalitarian relationship in some areas, but Fred was at a definite disadvantage in money matters, in part because he had no income except SSI. Kathryn who had cared for her aunt during the last three years of her aunt's life of ninety-five years inherited all of her aunt's land. The land with three producing gas wells, brought in considerable income, especially during boom times. This was money that Kathryn spent as she pleased. She voiced her philosophy on the use of money in the following:

> "I give money to everybody, to relatives, to friends. That is just the way the Indian lives. He doesn't worry about tomorrow. He just thinks about today. I gave my daughter $250, and she turned around and bought food for all those people in the march--that group of Indians that's walkin' to Washington's at Grand Junction now." Mary Pat was helping to collect shoes and coats for them, 'cause it's been snowin'. They missed one bill, but they plan to be in Washington by the end of July when the most important one is comin' up. Some movie stars and the Catholics are helpin' 'em. The Catholics always have a place for them to stay in the next town.

Mary Pat, Kathryn and Fred's youngest daughter, was also very involved in tribal politics, and she had the same philosophy that her mother and grandmother had about helping people. She graduated from the University of New Mexico and entered law school in Denver. She wanted to earn a law degree so that she could advise Indians on legal matters and represent them in court. After experiencing first-hand the discrimination against Indians on the march to Washington D.C., she recalled the many experiences of prejudice in her home town of Hammon and said, "If I had gone to law school before I wouldn't have been dedicated like I am now. I'm matured and I'm more dedicated now. I want to do something to help my people." Sadly she never had a chance. Mary Pat met an untimely death in an automobile accident in 1984.

Politics in the Hoffman household was very interesting. Fred was living in a household in which two women, as recipients of most of the income, were in complete control in money matters. The philosophy of his wife was exactly like that of his mother--share with everybody. Fred complained about his mother's generosity: "Mama has a lot a land. She has her mother's, her father's, and her sister's land. And she's always givin' her money away. When she gets her lease money, somebody's always askin' her for two hundred or one hundred dollars. They just line up. Then when they get their money they forget to pay her back. Myself, I'm gettin' kinda selfish. I have to look out for myself."

Fred, as Vinnie's only child, expected to inherit his mother's property, but Vinnie had not yet made a will in 1977, and she had other plans, "I'm gonna make a will and give five acres to Fred. That's what he's on and then another hundred and sixty, I'll give one-hundred sixty acres to the eight grandchildren, and another forty to the great-grandchildren."

Vinnie, in her old age, became mistrustful of her family and questioned their motives. After she sold some land a few years later, the money by some oversight had not been placed in an account for her sole use, and it disappeared quickly. Then she received forty-three thousand dollars for a five-year lease of her land, and Fred put five thousand of it in a savings account, which upset her. When Albert died, Fred then took money out of the savings account to pay funeral expenses. He said, "See, Mama, you can trust me. I did the right thing 'cause now that money can be used to pay for Papa's funeral."

Vinnie did not argue with Fred, but she said, "I do my own business now. I don't trust 'em." As much as possible, she did take care of her own business affairs. She had a lot of business to conduct. Her land, which soared in value in the 1970s and 1980s, brought in a considerable amount of income. But in spite of the fact that her income was five to ten times higher than that of the average Hammon Cheyenne family, her style of living gave no clue except through her generosity. Her small frame house, built fifty years ago, was in dire need of repair, as were most of the other Cheyenne houses. She rode in an old car belonging to her son or a grandson. She never spent money on anything for herself, but instead shared all she had with relatives and friends. As a potential benefactor to every member of the family, she was careful to analyze the sincerity of every need that came to her attention.

Vinnie was not quite sure how to interpret a grandchild's decision to bring his family to live in Hammon after her husband, Albert, died. In fact, she felt insulted when they said they wanted to take care of her. She often remarked, "I'm a big shot. I don't depend on nobody."

Vinnie Hoffman. Photo 1982. Courtesy, Wanda Queenan

She not only thought that she had to guard her money but also a valuable file of old Cheyenne tales that she had collected. Shortly after 1900 she had written down quite a few stories that had been passed down from grandparents and parents for several generations. Some family members wanted the stories to sell, a request that she refused. Although she kept them in an old trunk, she was very distressed when she discovered several missing. Her concern was that some family member, not a stranger, had taken them. The incident was a reminder that she could trust almost no one. In spite of the fact that Fred and Kathryn were very considerate of Vinnie's feelings and made every effort to show their affection by taking care of her wishes and needs, Vinnie remained mistrustful, perhaps because she had a considerable inheritance to pass on to the next generation.

In the later part of his life, Fred was more respected than at any other time. His family thoroughly enjoyed his companionship and showed him respect, a marked contrast to the earlier years. His days of irresponsibility belonged to the past. He was very proud of his achievements in trying to improve Cheyenne life. Fred believed that the most important contribution he and his family could make was to fight for Indian justice in a white man's world and preserve Cheyenne identity because "the Great Creator blessed us the same way he blessed the white man."

Vinnie died in 1989 at the age of ninety-five, Fred died in 1995, and Kathryn was still living at age ninety in August 2007.

Chapter Seven

ANNA CORNSTALK REYNOLDS HART, TEPEE MAKER, FAMILY

Anna Cornstalk Reynolds Hart, Tepee Maker, was born near Cantonment in the western section of the Cheyenne Arapaho Reservation in 1876. In spite of the fact that she was part Arapaho and part French, she always considered herself to be Cheyenne. Cornstalk, a great-great-grandmother in 1974, was one of the oldest and most respected women in Hammon. She was a very respected medicine woman who was frequently sought by other members of the tribe to treat a variety of ailments. In addition, she was the principal midwife for women of the Hammon Cheyenne community.

Among her many talents was bead working, an artistic and economic endeavor at which she was quite skilled and fast, enabling her to easily sell her work for a profit. Lawrence commented, "She supported my grandpa." She also was a tepee maker, a special designation for an important, well-respected woman in the tribe. When she made a tepee, she invited other women to join her. It was the job of her very young grandson, Sam, to carry water to the tepee where the women gathered, to keep the fire burning, and to stir the pot of food that the women would consume, a job he was proud to have.

Cornstalk married Peace Chief John Peak Heart, a Cheyenne who was born in 1872 to Afraid of Beavers and Walking Woman, four years after the Battle of the Washita. After spending his childhood in Hammon, he attended the Haskell Institute in Lawrence, Kansas. It was a fortuitous time because his attendance at the school coincided with the advent and subsequent sweep across the Plains by the Peyote religion, a religion that would become the most important and widespread Indian religion of the twentieth century. Its center was the Great Plains where the majority of Indians lived. As many as fifty percent of the Haskell students embraced the new religion that was incorporated under the name, Native American Church, but was also called the Peyote Cult and Church of the First Born. It was a religion that had an intellectual appeal especially to the young men imprisoned for three years at Ft. Marion, Florida. There, as Stewart (1987: 101) points out, the majority of prisoners were Cheyenne, and they were the first of the Plains Indians to learn the English language and to be instructed in the Christian religion. According to Stewart, English and Christianity were important precipitating factors in the rapid spread of the Peyote religion.

John Peak and Cornstalk had one son, Homer, and two daughters, Blanche and Lucy. The overriding interest, as the Hart family grew in number, was an education for each child. The parents transmitted to their children a belief that life without an education was hard and Cheyenne life without an education was very hard.

Homer finished grade school at Red Moon and then entered the Haskell Institute in Lawrence, Kansas. At an early age, he was fully committed to the Mennonite religion. He became a Mennonite missionary and was transferred to the Red Moon Mission in April 1916. Homer's sister Blanche married Henry White Shield, and Lucy, the youngest sister, unfortunately, contracted tuberculosis in her youth and died at the young age of seventeen. As she lay dying, Pastor Linscheid and a medicine man had a heated argument over whether or not she should be baptized. The missionary won, and Lucy was baptized three days before her death. Her mother, Cornstalk, was baptized later that day and her father twenty-three years later (Linscheid 1973: 159–162). It is very interesting that the father, John Peak, and the son, Homer, were advocates and missionaries for such seemingly opposing religious philosophies.

One day Howling Water rode his horse to the Mennonite mission and announced that someone in the night had stolen his beautiful daughter Jenny. He did not search for the person or say anything about the hat that the lover thief had dropped near his house in the night because he realized, without commenting, that Homer was the thief who had "stolen a bride," his daughter, and had taken her to his tepee. Jenny Howling Water and Homer Hart were now a married Indian couple. One month later, the couple asked for a Christian wedding (Ibid.). Jenny was described by Linscheid as "beautiful, with smooth copper colored skin, shiny black braids, and big dark eyes."

Jenny and Homer Hart. Courtesy, Lawrence Hart.

Jenny Howling Water Hart and Homer Hart thereafter became committed lay ministers for Mennonite churches in western Oklahoma. They both served for forty years. Homer held services, conducted funerals, and served as interpreter for those who did not know English, and Jenny taught Sunday School, planned the Christmas program, and assisted with women's activities. Jenny was very talented artistically. She played the organ, and she was a very skillful bead worker. She and Homer had six children: Sam, Alvin, Lawrence, Christine, Ramona, and Lenora.

When Lawrence was born, he was sent to live with his grandparents, Cornstalk and John Peak, for the first six years of his life, because his mother was very ill and could not care for him (WOHP MJW RH January 14, 1999). Lawrence reminisced about his experience in the following:

> Soon after I was born my mother became ill to the point that my paternal grandparents took me and reared me until I was age six or was nearing age six. Because my grandparents had essentially reared me as well, I was their grandson—but it was like I was their son, and I have learned since that when I reached age six, or was nearing age six, my parents knew that I needed to be in school. So what they did was, even though the grandparents who took care of me were a part of the family, they went through a proper custom and prepared some gifts and took them to my grandparents when they came after me to finally take me back as my parents and to then enroll me in a local rural one room school.

During the six years that Lawrence lived with his grandparents, he formed deep, lifelong relationships with each of them. Treated like a special son, Lawrence would always refer to his grandparents in affectionate terms. Every summer he and his grandmother, Cornstalk, accompanied John Peak on the annual peyote trip that was located on the Ute Reservation in the Four Corner's small town of Towaoc, Colorado. As a missionary for the Native American Church, John Peak went there for a period of three months every year for thirty-five years to teach the Half Moon ritual of the Peyote religion to the Utes. This was a major event because, in the past, the two tribes had been traditional enemies. John Peak was an important peace chief, one of the Forty-Four Peace Chiefs of the Northern and Southern Cheyennes. The office of peace chief was an honored position that required a commitment to non-violence.

Lawrence attended Bethel College in Newton, Kansas, for two years before becoming a fighter pilot in the U.S. Air Force, during which time he was notified that his grandfather was passing the mantle of peace chief of the Cheyenne to him. That is when he had his epiphany. Strongly influenced by his friend from Bethel College, who died while serving as a missionary in the Congo, Lawrence accepted the challenge to be a peacemaker, no matter what the cost, and to live it, to teach it, and to commit his life to nonviolence. Moral power would come from turning the other cheek, not from an act of revenge. In selecting Lawrence to take his place, John Peak gave Lawrence the ultimate honor. Lawrence commented that he strongly believed that his grandfather had been grooming him to be peace chief from Lawrence's early childhood years.

Cornstalk was selected to be Tepee Maker, a special honor bestowed by the tribe. She also was an expert gardener, and she took great pride in growing prize-winning vegetables. Betty, who was married to Lawrence, also excelled in the planting, growing, and harvesting of potatoes, carrots, beans, corn, cabbage, and beets. Cornstalk canned, a skill that the home economic clubs had been trying to teach some women, but for the most part, unsuccessfully. The two Hart families were awarded prizes for their produce. One time they won a pig that they shared with their neighbors. Cornstalk also raised chickens.

Sam remembered well the times:

> when a farmer would call us to tell us that one of their livestock had died and they'd give it to us. Grandfather and I would hitch up the team of horses and we'd go get the beef. We'd cut it up on the site and then bring it home. My grandmother would then slice the beef and hang it out to dry—that's the beef we had throughout the winters. It seems my grandmother was always concerned about other families. She knew how desperate they were, or how hungry. Those were the words she used: "How hungry they are." She'd invite them and she'd give

them beef, and all that hard work, you know. Sometimes we'd just have a little pile of beef left for us. She'd give it all away.

Cornstalk and John Peak were progressive agriculturalists, who put forth a concerted effort to make a living from their allotment, a goal they were able to achieve. Having some equipment, specifically a new combine, they harvested their own wheat relatively quickly, and then helped their neighbors harvest their wheat as well.

Lawrence is the executive director of the Cheyenne Culture Center located east of Clinton, Oklahoma, and his wife, Betty, is his assistant. Lawrence has many projects but the two most significant are his work as co-director of the Circle Keepers, an organization to educate and help the Cheyenne from preschool age to age eighteen to remain drug- and alcohol-free. The other project is Lawrence's national campaign to retrieve Indian bones held by museums and other third parties. The bones are to be returned to the appropriate tribe to be reburied.

Nathan, Lawrence and Betty's son, has a college degree from Bethel. In addition to holding a large number of local and national Indian offices, he is an excellent wood artist. Their daughter, Connie, earned a master's degree from Purdue and a law degree from Oklahoma City University. She has served as a federal judge. In 2007 she was a dance coordinator and in charge of the annual Red Earth Festival, which is a highly successful three-day Indian festival held in Oklahoma City. Indians come from almost every state in the union dressed in elaborately decorated clothing to participate in Indian dance contests and sell their handcrafted pieces of art and jewelry.

The Hart family has been more successful than other families in escaping the poverty trap in Hammon mainly because they place a high value on education, one that furnishes skills that lead to job opportunities. This is a value that can be traced back to Cornstalk.

John Peak continued his missionizing until he retired in 1950. He died at the age of eighty-eight in 1958, but Cornstalk lived until 1975 when she died at the age of one hundred two.

Chapter Eight

EMMA LOU STANDING WATER HART FAMILY

Emma Lou Standing Water Hart was eighty-four in January 2008. She was born to Merriam and Russell Standing Water, near Butler, Oklahoma, a small Custer County town a few miles east of Hammon. She married a grandson of Anna Cornstalk Hart, Alvin, and became a sister-in-law of his siblings, Lawrence, Sam, and Lenora. She grew up with stories about her great grandmother, White Buffalo Woman, who told her about the Cheyenne trek across the Plains. Emma Lou especially liked the story of the Battle of the Washita when her great-grandmother was taken prisoner. Emma Lou recalled:

> On that fateful night, my great-grandmother heard the crier call out, "Run and leave all your things." They put on their robes, my grandmother and my great-grandmother—their buffalo robes, and started running. In the rush my great-grandmother fell down in the tall grass on the riverbank, and she stayed there to hide. Then she heard someone say, "Run. Save your life." She said, "I've been hit." She could hear those horses coming. The soldiers found her and took her prisoner. My grandma would never take her moccasins off at night after that. Someone asked her why, and she said, "I might have to run in the night."

Emma Lou Standing Water Hart.

After she and Alvin Hart were married, he enlisted in the military service, and the two of them moved to Texas where he was first stationed. Emma Lou recalled: "Later we got to go to Germany. All of the Hart boys went to the service. Alvin had one sister, Lenora, and she married a service man so she got to go some place too."

Alvin was transferred many times during his twenty-three years of military service to bases mostly in the southwest—Wichita, Kansas; Wichita Falls, Texas; San Antonio, Texas, among others. So many moves were not easy with a growing family. The Hart family was growing by one every year or two until there were nine children. Counting mother and father, the total number of family members was eleven.

Alvin had a heart attack in 1964, and he was given a medical discharge. He and Emma Lou moved with their children back to Hammon, and enrolled those who had not yet graduated from high school in the Hammon Public Schools.

Alvin and Emma Lou were never very happy about the school. Emma Lou was particularly sensitive about the ongoing discrimination against Indian students at the school. She pointed out that, at all the white schools her children had attended with white children, in various locations, her children never experienced any problem with prejudice until they got to Hammon.

In the 1970s when the new Institute of the Southern Plains became a possible school choice for Hammon Cheyenne children, Emma Lou agreed to teach two classes in the Cheyenne language. When there was a dispute over whether or not the school should remain open, she led the protest against the dissenters who were against the new Indian school and wanted it closed.

Alvin was a peace chief, the only one in the Hammon area for a short time in the seventies, which was a true honor. His health declined and he became weaker. In 1976 he had a massive heart attack that killed him.

Emma Lou has endured a hard life, but she always has a smile on her face. Of the nine children born to her and Alvin, only six of them were still living in March 2006. She is very proud of her eight grandchildren, but expressed dismay and bewilderment at their genders. Only one was a girl and seven were boys.

Five young grandchildren and great-grandchildren plus a resident granddaughter, Lelah, were living in Emma Lou's home in the spring of 2006. Lelah was the mother of the two boys, ages two and five, who were in Emma Lou's care during the day while Lelah worked the early morning shift at a restaurant. She started at seven a.m., and finished at about two-thirty in the afternoon. In addition, Emma Lou took responsibility for two grandsons, ages fifteen and seventeen, whose father, was killed in a car accident in Montana and whose mother remained there. The boys did not want to return to Montana. They wanted to live with their grandmother. Three being in school all day lessened her responsibility, but she had all five after school, at night, and for breakfast, until summer.

Emma Lou's daughter's son was an eighth-grader who slept and ate at his grandmother's house because he preferred living in Hammon to living in Clinton. To make things a little more difficult, at eighty-two Emma Lou not only had her age working against her in the role of surrogate mother of five, but she also had diabetes, a devastating disease that is widespread among American Indians. She is also a stomach cancer survivor. Being the chief babysitter has not been easy for her physically or psychologically. But relatively speaking, she does not have to worry as much as others because she has regular income and her house is paid for.

She lamented that she no longer had income from beading because beading causes cramping in her hands. With sadness she stated, "I don't bead anymore. My hands catch cramps. I wish I could bead. My granddaughter said, 'Just go ahead and bead.' I started beading and my hands just cramped."

She paid off the mortgage on her house last year bringing her a great sense of relief. The house needs considerable repairs, but since she lives so far from the BIA headquarters, she can only request and hope that the BIA will finally reach her house. She spends her pension money on utilities and on groceries for the six resident family members of her house. Her daughter drives her to the Altus Air Force base commissary once every month where she can save about ten to fifteen percent on her grocery bill. She is entitled to shop there because of her husband's military service. Emma Lou's son, who lives in Colorado, sends her money from time to time, which helps considerably.

Emma Lou senses a great void in her life. Her husband died thirty years ago, and she has been in charge of the family since. It seems to her as if all the men in her family and everyone else's family are gone. In her words, "We don't hardly have any men folks around. They're all gone. All my people are gone. I only have two first cousins. One lives in Elk City and one lives in Anadarko. All my friends are dying. Blanche White Shield who was ninety-one, died a month ago and now I don't have anybody to talk to. I used to talk to her almost every day on the phone. But we all have to die. I wish I could hurry and die. It would get me out of my misery."

Emma Lou fell two weeks before my last visit with her in April 2006. Her body was badly bruised, especially her arm, that had a large swollen knot about the size of a lemon. Her family got a walker for her, but she lamented, "It don't do much good. The grandkids like to play with it and they have it." So when she has periods of instability and doesn't have access to her walker, she is in danger of falling. Her family recognized that she was not able to care for the small children at least for awhile, so they made other arrangements for the children's day care.

With the summer beginning and school ending, there was some concern about the older boys not having jobs. Since their father died, they had been getting Social Security checks, and they said that they couldn't work because they would get too much money and be penalized by the government. But Emma Lou had plenty of jobs around her house that they could at least help with.

She is especially proud of her grandson. Not only is he a graduating senior, but he also is salutatorian of his senior class, a real achievement and honor for any boy or girl, but for a Cheyenne Indian, it is very special. He enrolled in college classes at Southwestern State College in Weatherford, Oklahoma, for the fall of 2006, and he lived in the dorm, a good sign that he was planning to stay.

Emma Lou was happy to have her grandchildren as resident family members, but she was not quite sure how it all had happened. She said, shaking her head, "I have children with parents, but the children live with me."

Part Three

Rural Community

Cornstalk and John Peak Hart. Courtesy Lawrence Hart

Chapter Nine

BEADING, GENDER, AND LIVELIHOOD

Adornment with beads can be traced back nearly 75,000 years to South Africa, (Wong: 2006: 76). It was well known to all indigenous peoples who had access to a variety of materials, in varying degrees of abundance, that were ideal for beading. This included shells, bones, stones, seeds, and animal teeth.

When Europeans brought glass beads to trade for Indian goods, beading became very popular in many tribes. Cheyennes were quickly attracted to the trade beads and enthusiastically began bartering pelts, horses, and essential food items for the tiny beads. The first European beads were white and imperfect in finish but were highly valued. The brightly-colored trade beads that followed soon adorned almost every item of clothing the Cheyennes wore--shirts, dresses, moccasins, belts, headdresses--as well as other items, such as parfleches, cradle boards, tepees, and ceremonial items.

Today the production of beaded items comprises almost the entire economy of the Hammon Cheyennes. Engaged in primarily by women, Cheyenne beadwork is a critical resource of income for many Indian families, and it often means the difference between eating and not eating.

Beading skills provided Cheyenne women with an opportunity to develop an economic enterprise. A woman's beading proficiency and productivity were so important that beadwork could bring her not only significant prestige, but financial rewards as well. The very skilled bead workers were the most respected women in the tribe and were rewarded by being designated to make special tepees and ceremonial items.

Cheyenne–Arapaho Bead Workers. Photo 1900, no. 19383.90.1 Barde Collection. Courtesy, Research Division of the Oklahoma Historical Society.

One of the expert bead workers also was likely to be asked to fill a special order of beadwork from the outside world. Martha Fingernail disbelievingly recalled, "One day two months ago things were really bad. A white woman came and ordered a buckskin dress. I had never made one, but I tried, and I finished it in five days, and she paid five hundred dollars for it." Martha knew that it was a once in a lifetime happening.

Women who bead are extremely proud of their skill and talk about how they learned it from their mothers or grandmothers. Lillie Elk River Hayes was one of the more accomplished bead workers in Hammon, having decorated five tepees, many dresses, and more moccasins than she could remember. The most usual source of money in times of scarcity was the sale of beadwork. Anna Hawk told many stories about beadwork that had enabled her to get through a financial crisis. Highly skilled bead workers, Anna, Lillie, Kathryn, and Cornstalk were four among the Cheyenne women in the community who could make a profit from their work, that is, if they could get the finished beadwork to market where it commanded a high price. Locally beadwork was not readily marketable because of low demand. Public transportation was expensive and could cut a meager profit in half.

One day when Anna Hawk's family was desperate for money, she made the decision to sell a pair of her own fully beaded moccasins. She knew that she had a better chance than anyone in the family to produce the money needed. She used public transportation to travel to a store that would pay cash for her fully beaded moccasins. Her travel cost was twenty-five dollars for a round-trip bus fare and ten dollars for two taxi fares (the nearest bus station was eighteen miles away). Considering the cost of materials, a seventy-five dollar sale price for the moccasins left her only forty dollars as compensation for the many hours she had spent beading. But, at the time, she had no choice in the matter because no other family member had the means to help.

The greater portion of the twenty-five Cheyenne women bead workers in Hammon in 1975 were members of the oldest generation living. In the second oldest generation only fifteen to twenty percent of women beaded because most preferred domestic work, Cheyenne agency jobs, or menial jobs, if available, that paid little but more than they could earn from beading. These women regarded beading as a supplemental skill and had little interest in learning to spend many long hours for a small return.

The consequence is that the skill may disappear in a few generations if young Cheyenne women are not interested in keeping the artistry of beading alive. Irene Hayes lamented, "I don't bead. I can do a little. I thought that my grandmother [Lillie] was going to live forever and that I didn't need to learn. She used to tell me to sit down and she would tell me how she was going to do this, and she would show me, and I just didn't listen. I'd sit there to please her for just a minute, and then I would get up and go."

Beading special items is considered to be a spiritual endeavor. Typically the woman who is planning to bead goes through a lengthy ritual of prayer before she begins. Beading in the earlier years was considered to be a female activity, and men were not allowed to come near, a reverse philosophy of the gender prohibition of women in or near the Arrow Ceremony.

The young woman who learned to bead became an apprentice to a skilled bead worker who taught the basic techniques of beading. If the woman excelled in learning the craft, she could then ask permission to duplicate her mentor's designs. The women who beaded were divided into units in which all of the participants had attained a similar level of expertise. As the students became proficient, they advanced to a more skilled group with higher standards, much like the workers' guilds in medieval Europe. It was a system of apprenticeship that over time acquired a reputation for exclusiveness.

The historical division of labor that assigned beading to women has weakened in today's economy. Men seldom beaded in the past, and when they did, they beaded ceremonial items only. Women always did the greatest amount of beading and continue to do so today, and they mostly bead moccasins, the items that generate the most income. Men in the past were only willing to add soles to the moccasins because beading was "women's work." Now that beading is a readily available source of money, it is regarded more favorably. If men can ignore the teasing from other men, they may start beading. A few men have already begun, and they tend to be very fast bead workers.

In the year 2004, according to the U.S. BIA, 5,700 of the 9,729 Cheyennes and Arapahos living in or adjacent to the tribes' eight-county region in Oklahoma were available for the work force. The unemployment rate of that available work force was sixty-six percent and of those employed, thirty-three percent were living below the poverty line. In Hammon, the statistics are worse because teachers, teachers' aides, and city workers have the only permanent jobs in the town, and those are government funded. Most of the jobs Cheyennes have outside the town are jobs that are government-created or government-funded. Tribal councilmen, employees of the Committee of Concerns, a committee created to deal with Cheyenne social problems, teachers, and teachers' aides are paid with government funds.

Indian poverty rates have been and continue to be considerably higher than poverty rates for the general population. In the year 2000 the percentage of the United States population living below the poverty line was 12.4 percent, but for Cheyennes and Arapahos in western Oklahoma, it was 42.3 percent. Specifically, 4,808 individual Cheyennes and Arapahos and 913 Cheyenne and Arapaho families were living below the poverty line. In Cheyenne and Arapaho households with a female head and no male present, the number of persons in poverty climbed to sixty-five percent (USDOC 2000).

The mean earnings of Hammon Cheyennes from all sources in 2004 were derived from government assistance—Old Age Pensions, Aid to the Blind, Aid to the Disabled, Aid to Families with Dependent Children, veterans' benefits, and a few Social Security checks. The mean earnings of Hammon Cheyennes in 2004 was $31,333. The Social Security mean was $7,702, the Supplemental Security mean was $5,618, the public assistance mean was $3,034, and the retirement mean was $11,930 (Ibid.).

Unemployment numbers in Hammon run very high in winter months, sometimes as high as ninety percent. Government jobs are almost the only full time jobs available for the local Cheyennes. The biggest employer in the area is the public school that regularly has jobs for white and Indian teachers' aides, and sometimes a teacher position. One Cheyenne held a job in county maintenance, which is a government paid job. The other employer is the farmer's co-op that hires seasonally.

The BIA office at Concho aids approximately seventy-five percent of families who are waiting to qualify for its various programs. Assistance ranges from $200 to $750 per family per month (CAR 1973). The BIA also has an emergency assistance fund to help pay rents, utilities, medical costs, and funeral expenses. It also supplies food vouchers for those who do not qualify for the food distribution program and childcare. It sponsors a program disseminating medical information to tribal members and gives financial assistance. It also provides funds for college scholarships, adult education, and the Head Start program.

BIA funds are distributed on EA Day, or Emergency Assistance Day, the day when members of the Cheyenne–Arapaho Tribes visit elected officials seeking emergency assistance money from the month's tribal casino profits. A business committee member estimates that eighty percent of the profit from the casinos is given to individual members for emergencies on a first come first served basis (*DO* May 9, 2004).

Food, and particularly healthy food, for Cheyennes has always been scarce. After the monthly food stamps are gone, people either borrow from each other or go without, because only a few of them have a job. Some of the men have part-time jobs on nearby ranches, but they are generally poorly paid, and as recently as the 1950s and 1960s, often their pay was in goods only.

To alleviate the scarcity of food problem today, once each month the U.S. Department of Agriculture's commodity program issues commodities to households with incomes below the poverty line. In addition to flour, cornmeal, rice, and beans, there are canned meats, fruits, vegetables, and dried milk.

In the 1950s the government devised a plan to eliminate Indian poverty by relocating unemployed Cheyennes to urban areas with greater employment opportunities and training them in vocational skills. The plan was largely unsuccessful. Although it was a belated official recognition that Indians could not be farmers because their land holdings were too minimal or nonexistent, it still did not take into consideration the strong communal approach to life practiced and preferred by the individual Indian.

Not only did land ownership slip away from Indians, but what land they kept brought in a decreasing share of lease or royalty money. The system of inheritance resulted in an extreme fractionalization of land holdings so that all the heirs of a deceased owner would share in the income derived from leases on the land allotment. A few allotments were transferred to individual owners, but most were transferred to a number of heirs. Of the original two hundred allotments made to Cheyennes and Arapahos in this area in 1891, only thirty (or fifteen percent) were still owned by Indians in 1978. Some allotments might have only five heirs, but others would have as many as one hundred twenty-five. Annual income for individuals from these leases in most cases amounted to no more than one hundred dollars, and in many cases only ten or twenty dollars. One Indian family received as little as sixteen cents per person per year.

A little more than half of the Cheyennes in Hammon over age fifty receive some income from land leases. As noted these amounts can vary a great deal. There is often rivalry between children and grandchildren who are eager to inherit a share of this land. Living with and taking care of a person in his or her last days gives a preeminent right to inherit. Ed Whiteskunk, who inherited 160 acres of land from his grandmother, stated: "I lived with my grandmother, took care of her, and did things for her. When she died she gave me her land. She liked me. The others were mad because they didn't get anything, but I was the one who took care of her."

Housing conditions improved slowly but minimally. By the time World War I broke out, only a few Cheyennes had moved to houses in town, but the houses were substandard frame houses covered with cardboard or boards from orange crates, and most continued to live in canvas tents. The move from camps on the river to houses did not begin in earnest until 1958. By approximately 1965, at least half of the Indians lived in town. With the exception of a few older Indians, who stayed on the river until they died, most of the remaining ones moved in 1968 when each Cheyenne received tribal claim checks of $2,300 as a result of a claim that the Indian Claims Commission had settled for them. This disbursement was also given to the Southern Arapahos.

The very low subsistence level provided by the Cheyenne economy in the river camp improved in many respects with the move to town. On the river camp housing was virtually free, food sources were more obtainable, wood was always available to make a fire, and there were no heat and light bills to pay. The move to town transformed the Cheyenne economy into a welfare economy, a government plan that backfired according to Kathryn Hoffman because "when the Indians started sellin' their allotments, they didn't have nothin' to live off of. They started movin' to town and livin' in houses. Now they have nothin'. Today everybody's on welfare."

Poor quality housing has been an on-going problem throughout the Indian community. In 1973 the Bureau of Indian Affairs reported that eighty-five percent of the homes would be labeled substandard with between one-third and one-half of the homes being totally non-repairable. The heating in many homes was inadequate or potentially dangerous, and almost one-half had inadequate or no toilet facilities. Over half of the houses showed high degrees of rat, fly, and roach infestation (CAR 1973: 5).

The spending of tribal money has always been controversial. One group believes that money in the tribal treasury should be distributed per capita, while others believe that a good portion of that money should be used for tribal programs, i.e. development, emergency food distributions, housing improvements, senior programs, and lobbying Congress to return tribal lands to the tribe.

The sources of tribal money are varied. First is money awarded the tribe from the U.S. government for treaty violations and past grievances. In 1961 the Indian Claims Commission awarded the Cheyenne–Arapaho Tribes 23.5 million dollars for treaty violations, half of which was for the Southern Cheyennes and Arapahos. In 1968 $2,325 from the Judgment Fund was distributed to each of 5,323 adults on the Southern Cheyenne tribal roll. Opportunists (many from out of state) with goods to sell, descended on the town, selling anything they could, for the cash that was being distributed. Indians spent the money on many different things. Some used it to buy one of the houses in town. By combining payments of several persons, a house purchase was feasible. Others bought cars, lawn mowers, appliances, and an assortment of many things. By nightfall not much money was left in Cheyenne hands.

A second source of revenue comes from the bingo halls and the smoke shops in Concho and Clinton. The smoke shops do quite well because customers do not have to pay state tax on goods bought on tribal land. This tax amounts to a considerable sum because Oklahoma has a high tax on gas and cigarettes. The smoke shops, the bingo halls, and the casinos combined employ approximately two hundred and fifty people and could provide job opportunities for the Hammon Indians. The reality is that Hammon Indians have no public transportation available and no credit to buy any kind of vehicle. They live too far away to take advantage of these new employment opportunities. Also, the Cheyennes working in tribal positions in Clinton need employment as much as the Hammon Cheyennes do.

As of July 2006, the state of Oklahoma had seventy-eight of the eighty-four casinos in the Kansas, Texas, Oklahoma region. The initial revenues from the Cheyenne and Arapaho casinos were considerably higher than predicted and, as recently as 2005, were increasing dramatically. The tribes pay the state between two and six percent of their net revenue, and the remainder goes to the tribes for economic development and other programs. The outlook for the future of the casino source of money is not assured because of looming competition that will, no doubt, draw customers away from the Cheyenne Lucky Star Casinos. Remington Park Racetrack, located in Oklahoma City, has opened a six-hundred fifty game casino, and vastly larger casinos have been completed on I-35 south of Norman, Oklahoma. Further competition comes from the Chickasaws who have turned their Newcastle, Oklahoma, casino into a permanent building (*DO* August 27, 2005).

A third source of revenue comes from the oil wells located on tribal land. Oil companies lease these properties from the tribes and pay royalty to the tribes on all oil and gas removed. Some income is also derived from farming activities—the sale of grains, hay, cotton, and cattle raised and nourished on tribal lands and leasing pasturage for cattle belonging to other farmers (USDA 1969).

Government programs designed to train Cheyennes in employable skills have largely been failures. Furthermore, income no longer exists to replace former income derived from leasing allotments. In 1972 CETA, the Comprehensive Education and Training Act, provided a program in which the government paid salaries to employees while they trained for regular jobs. Even though it provided free labor to the employer for the period of three months, only a very few Indians were hired permanently. They either declined the job offer, or the employer did not ask them to stay and keep the job.

Lack of transportation and poor health create almost insurmountable barriers to steady employment. The State Employment Service in Clinton, Oklahoma, estimates that seventy per cent of Indians in Hammon are unemployable. To compound the problem, local townspeople and farmers refuse to hire anyone who is suspected of being a "radical Indian" or an "activist."

With no assets, very little income, and bad or no credit, an Indian in need of money is lucky to be able to obtain a loan anywhere. Before 1976 the only person or institution willing to loan money to a Hammon Cheyenne required that the applicant's house be used as collateral. By failing to make payments, paying in cash, failing to get a receipt, or having one and losing it, the unfortunate Indian looses his or her house to the bank. The house then is sold to someone who will rent it to the same or another Indian family. Anna Hawk alleged that between 1970 and 1976 five Indian families lost their houses because the bank had foreclosed on their loans.

Higher rates of mortality and illness and shorter life spans for Indians, are the direct results of Indian economic and social problems, and they magnify the effects of the fundamental differences in living standards of Indians and whites. As far back as the data extend, mortality rates have been consistently higher for the Cheyenne than for whites. Although the death rate of the Indian population has decreased markedly since 1900, there is still today a considerable difference in age-specific death rates of Indian and white populations. All Oklahoma Indians in the age bracket spanning the first forty-four years of life have a death rate two and one-half to three times higher than that of the whole U.S. Between the ages of forty-five and seventy-four, Indians continue to have a higher rate. Then between seventy-five and eighty-four the mortality rates are much the same, and by the age of eighty-five there appears to be a "mortality cross-over." Indians by then have lower age specific mortality rates than whites (USC 1990).

Heap-of-Birds family.
Courtesy of the Research Division of the Oklahoma Historical Society.

Indian birth rates increased almost every year from 1968 to 2004. The overall fertility rate for American Indian women is lower that that for women in general. However, birth rates for young women are higher among American Indians than for women overall, and infant and child mortality rates for American Indians are higher than those for all infants and children (HHS).

Good health is an important factor for employability. Cancer, heart disease, and stroke that are among the main causes of death, are almost inevitable with so many, widespread high risk factors—tobacco and alcohol use, poor diet, and obesity. Diabetes is increasing at an alarming rate and is present in almost every Indian family. Its complications include kidney failure, amputations, blindness, and heart disease. A constant reminder of this dreaded disease is reflected in the number of overweight people and amputees.

Among young persons, especially men ages fifteen to twenty-five, accidents rank as the main cause of death, and alcohol continues to take a heavy toll on the entire tribe. Most notably, it can cause severe liver diseases—alcoholic hepatitis or cirrhosis, both of which can lead to an early death. Lacerations, abrasions, and fractures are commonly alcohol-related, and many car accidents in the area are attributable to alcohol. Alcohol is also responsible for fetal alcohol syndrome, a malformation caused by the consumption of alcohol during pregnancy that manifests itself in cranial, neural, and facial dysfunctions. And finally, alcohol is often the trigger of a suicide. Six of eight suicides that occurred between May 1973 and May 1974 were alcohol-induced. Anna Hawk declared, "Alcohol is the worst thing that ever happened to the Indian people."

Chapter Ten

"INDIANS KNEW GOD BEFORE
THE WHITE MAN"

The Indians used herbs and knew God and nature
before the white man came with the Bible and his God.
Then the Indian had to defend the rights of the Native
American Church and the rights of peyote. We call the
white people intruders. They brought in their religion,
their law and said it was the only one there was. They're
dictators. They want to do away with the Indian. They
want to terminate the Indian.

--Fred Hoffman

Native religion at the time of historical contact was an important
integrating force in Cheyenne culture. Religious attitudes and values
permeated every facet of life, no matter what the activity, whether
politics, medicine, subsistence activities, arts and crafts, recreation, even
family relationships. The Cheyenne were a deeply spiritual people whose
supernatural world was populated by gods and spirits that were present
in varying degrees in human beings, animals, and plants, as well as
in inanimate objects. The Cheyenne personified the natural elements,
trees, rocks, and certain birds and animals, and they believed that the
attributes of a particular bird or animal could be transferred to a person
or another animal or bird by possession of feathers, hides, bones, or any

part of the creature's body. Spirits and gods were imputed powers that could, if necessary, be invoked as aids, abetted, or neutralized by certain practices and rituals. Reverence for sacred symbols and the creation of those symbols were regarded as necessary to receive divine benefits and services and to ensure a trouble-free life.

The Cheyenne personification of the supernatural was manifest in the culture hero, Sweet Medicine, a real person who served as the link between the people and the Great Spirit, or Maheo. According to legend, Maheo created the Cheyenne earth and everything in it. He was above all the Cheyenne, and he worked his wonders through his prophet, Sweet Medicine. The story of Sweet Medicine follows:

> Many generations ago Sweet Medicine went into the Sacred Mountain (Bear Butte) in the Black Hills in South Dakota and met Maheo, who gave him four sacred arrows to take back to his people. Along with the arrows Sweet Medicine brought back the tribe's culture, its ceremonies, its moral and ethical values, and its social and political structure. The proper care of the arrows ensured the tribe prosperity and protected them from disaster. They were assured success on the hunt and protection from enemies. But in order to receive these benefits, they were to keep the arrows forever "sweet and clean." They were warned that the arrows would be besmirched if one Cheyenne killed another Cheyenne, and then the well being of the people would be at risk. Only banishment of the offender and the staging of a purification ritual of the arrows, would return the Cheyenne to a state of continued blessings (Llewellyn and Hoebel 1941:133–135).

Sweet Medicine predicted the coming of the white people and the demise of the Cheyenne in the following:

> A time is coming when you will meet other people. You will fight with them and kill each other. Each tribe will want the other tribe's land, and you will be fighting always… The buffalo will disappear. When the buffalo are gone, the next animal you eat will be spotted. When you get toward the end,

you will begin to become gray very young. You will marry even your relatives. You will reach a point where you will be ashamed of nothing, and you will act as if you were crazy. Soon you will find among you a people with hair all over their faces. Their skin will be white. When that time comes, they will control you. The white people will be all over the land; and at last you will disappear (Powell 1969: 466).

Cheyenne spiritual life was based on nature spirits. There were good and bad spirits. Of great concern were the spirits that were connected with danger or death. In early historical times, according to Grinnell (1923 2:105) eagles, ravens, hawks, and owls possessed supernatural power, particularly in matters concerning war, because they captured their prey and subsisted on the flesh. Feathers of these birds were highly prized by warriors. They communicated danger to their foe and power to the person who wore or carried them. The birds with colorful feathers— the red and yellow flickers, the magpie with its iridescent greenish-black tail, the scissor-tail, and others were greatly admired and collected to decorate clothing and religious paraphernalia. Anna Hawk recalled seeing the owl that proved to be a true ill omen:

> Me and my sister woke up one morning hearin' "Hoo-oo-oot, hoo-oo-oot, hoo-oo-oot." It was still kinda dark, and my father stepped outside and then began motionin' for us to come. And there in the big tree right next to the creek were four young owls. The sun wasn't up yet, but I could tell my father was scared. I knew what it meant. But there wasn't nothin' we could do about it. Two weeks later my mother died. The owl is always a bad sign. Sometimes when the owl comes, he asks for bread. He will say in Cheyenne, "Give me some bread." But he's a bad bird.

In the pre-reservation period, the Cheyenne warrior wearing a war bonnet of gray eagle feathers was believed to have been rendered invulnerable to bullets or arrows (Ibid. 108). An eagle feather, therefore, in the wrong hands was always a cause for alarm. The eagle was extremely potent, and its feathers could only be possessed by specific individuals who knew how to contain that power and direct it to good use. Finding and killing an eagle was exceptionally difficult because of the inaccessibility of its nest at extreme heights, and only when the eagle was in its deepest sleep. A Cheyenne who could accumulate eagle feathers was considered to be a very brave, highly skilled warrior.

Moses Starr (WOHP-LF March 26, 2001) explained the high regard the Cheyenne had for the eagle.

> The eagle meant a lot to us, and to us that's the most important bird because it is strong, it's keen in its sight, and it's the only bird from the earth that can go higher than any bird there is, and so we have a lot of respect for it. We use the feathers in our traditional dancing. We use the feather in our ceremonies. Every time we stop like in the Sun Dance and everyone has prayer and meditation to the Almighty set in their mind, then it never fails, that eagle will come. You can see him flying way up there, maybe two or three eagles, maybe just one. Then everybody looks and everything is all right.

The Cheyenne also used feathers of the hawk, and the red-headed woodpecker in their ceremonies. They considered the sighting of a cardinal to be good luck.

According to Lawrence Hart, trees were in a special category:

> Especially important were four kinds of native trees that were held sacred—the wild willow, the cedar, the dogwood, and the cottonwood. The cottonwood was the tree used for the lodge poles, and a lot of the family summer shades are willow. The dogwood was used in many ways. It was used to make the poles for the Sun Dance and other sacred ceremonies. The cedar is harvested, dried, and used as incense—the flat cedar not the Virginia cedar. It was used in the healing and the sacred ceremonies. Once a tree selection was made, the persons designated to cut it into appropriate sizes engaged in an informal conversation with the tree. The men told the tree what it was being used for, and they expressed their spiritual gratitude to the tree for being available to participate in the ceremony.

Spiritual communication with inanimate objects and living birds and animals was the very essence of the Cheyenne nature religion. All of nature, they believed, was filled with spirit beings that were somehow linked to the preservation of their existence, and it was believed to be a reciprocal relationship. The person would respect the spiritual source, whether it be a tree, a rock, or a feather from a bird, and in return, the source, the spirit being, would protect the person from harm, guide him or her to animals for the hunt, and protect him or her in battle or on a raid. The thought was, "I am a living being. I have a soul. I have a conscience. That tree is a living being also. It has a soul. It also has a conscience that protects me. It gives me spiritual guidance. I, in return, respect it. I bring it gifts. If I have to cut it down, I will honor it by using it for something important for both of us." The belief in a world populated with spirit beings that could communicate with humans was characteristic of all American Indian spiritual beliefs before contact with Christianity.

Upon exposure to European religions, some Indians quickly became followers and members of Protestant denominations or the Catholic Church. Others adopted Christianity in order to have additional spiritual help, and still others held fast to their old beliefs. Some Cheyenne were not frightened by the appearance of an occasional ill omen and privately acknowledged that some of these ancient beliefs were silly. In beliefs about the dead, for example, there was a contradiction in the ancient religion and the new. It was manifest in Cheyenne reverence, helplessness, and abnormal fear of anything connected with the dead on the one hand, and manifest by joking and perhaps a little irreverence as voiced by Anna Hawk:

> You know the Indians used to bury the dead on top of the ground laid on four poles stuck in the ground. Some were wrapped and hung from trees. And nobody was ever supposed to go there because somethin' really bad would happen to you. But when my mother was a little girl, she used to go to the burial grounds and pick up bracelets and rings. No one really knew who they belonged to because there were just a bunch of bones lying on the ground.

The burial always took place as far away from the camp as was practical. When the corpse was placed on the scaffold, the mourners took extensive measures to avoid being near or touching the dead and their possessions, including clothes, horses, and household goods. They also avoided mentioning the name of the dead in any capacity. They believed that the dead person's ghost hovered near the corpse and might seek revenge for some past misdeed. Even the tepee or lodge in which the deceased had lived was abandoned or destroyed to avoid contamination of the living. The Cheyenne fear of death and anything associated with death is very much like that of other Indians. But it was especially true of the Plains Apaches in Oklahoma and other Apaches who were mostly located in New Mexico and Arizona (Opler 1965; Opler and Bittle 1961).

From pre-reservation days up to the present, elaborate native ceremonies have been important community integrating forces—forces that are reinforced by the sacred circle and the sacred number four. The most sacred symbol in the Cheyenne world was the circle—the sun, the moon, the dance step, the camp circle, the tepee, the paths of the sun and the moon. All were circles that were replicated many times in ritual and artistic expressions. The circle confirmed one's equality and cooperation with others. It and the number four governed all Cheyenne rituals as it did in other Plains Indian traditions. Ritual groupings, the passing of the pipe, and blessings of the four arrows were all performed four times. Four songs were sung four times by four people. Movements within the circle always ran clockwise, repeating the path of the sun from east to west.

An atmosphere of excitement ran through the camp as time drew near for the summer ceremonies—the Arrow Ceremony, or Arrow Renewal, and the Sun Dance, both of which formed the core of Cheyenne spiritual life. These ceremonies were held annually when possible. Tragically the U.S. government outlawed the performance of American Indian ceremonies by any tribe from 1885 to 1934, forty-nine years, because they feared the Indians could cause serious trouble if allowed to gather in one place. The government operated under the premise that Indians would become civilized if they abandoned their pagan religion and converted to Christianity. It was especially true for the Plains Indians. Many of the ceremonies, however, were held with the local authorities' knowledge, or in secret in spite of the ban. After 1934 the Sun Dance, the Arrow Ceremony, and other ceremonies began to be revived and celebrated openly.

The Sacred Arrow ceremony and the Sun Dance were summer ceremonies that could be held annually, but not necessarily, and sometimes only one or the other was held. The purpose of the Sacred Arrow ceremony was to purify the four sacred arrows for use in the Sun Dance, so it usually came first when both were held. The organization of the ceremony was the responsibility of two people, the pledger, a person who was under duress of a threatened personal loss, and who expected to avert a tragic happening by his participation, and the instructor who was an older, experienced man.

Two of the arrows were designated buffalo arrows with the power to confuse buffalos, and render them easier to surround and kill. The other two arrows had power to weaken enemies into a vulnerable state. The Pawnees had stolen the four sacred arrows in 1830, and Cheyenne priests created replacement arrows. The Pawnees then returned the two buffalo arrows, but kept the two arrows that had power over human beings. The Cheyenne placed the two returned arrows with the four replacement arrows, bringing to a total of six the number of arrows that the bundle of arrows contained. The main misfortunes of the Cheyenne during the nineteenth century were directly attributed to the loss of the Sacred Medicine Arrows.

At the time of the summer solstice, the Cheyenne would gather for the ceremony of the Renewal of the Sacred Arrows. When the skin bundle containing the arrows was opened, Hoebel (1941) described it as: "the moment of supreme sacredness of the Cheyenne as a people. It was the moment at which the well being of the tribe as a whole was in the process of renewal. The Medicine Arrows symbolized the collective existence as a tribe. In a sense the arrows may be called the embodiment of the tribal soul." Ideally the Sacred Arrow Renewal and the Sun Dance were held annually, but when that was not possible the two were alternated.

The Arrow Ceremony was believed by some to be more powerful than the Sun Dance or the Peyote ritual, especially for illness. Eugene Blackbear (WOHP MJW July 15, 1999) explained the importance of having spiritual help with progressive levels of renewal available, especially for persons who were ill:

> First, we make a vow for somebody that's sick-- maybe put up a peyote meeting. And (if) it seem like that don't quite get 'em well, well like the way we want 'em to. Or maybe, it's kinda emergency, not too late, then that's when we use the other one, what they call another vow. This one goes a little bit higher— the Sun Dance, the peyote and the Sun Dance. Then if the Sun Dance don't work, then we have this last one, the Arrow worship. Got the four sacred arrows. And just the women, they bring gifts over. That's all. They don't be there when we do a little bit of ceremonial ways. The Arrow ceremony is mostly men, men's religion. Women cannot have a part.

Hammon Cheyennes, even today, attend one or two of the annual Sun Dances in the north central part of the U.S. Pastor Max Malone estimated that about one-half of the tribe goes to the Northern Cheyenne Sun Dance in Montana, and the other half travel to Wyoming for the Arapaho Sun Dance, because some Cheyennes are married to Arapahos or have Arapaho friends. The Southern Cheyenne's Sun Dance is normally held at Seiling, Oklahoma.

The purpose of the Sun Dance ritual today is primarily social, although for some the experience is still spiritual. Native rituals provide some of the few socially approved outlets for pent-up frustrations of being Indian, which is why Martin Fingernail attended all the native rituals when he was in Hammon. In response to the question of how he coped with the widespread discrimination in Hammon, he replied: "I'm Indian. I go to Sun Dances and pray to Sweet Medicine. I do the Arrow Ceremony. I fast and then I have visions. I have visions about everything that's happenin' here, [the maltreatment]. I just want to be treated like a human being."

Christianity was introduced into the Cheyenne community in the late nineteenth century after Cheyennes had been confined to the reservation. In 1869 President Ulysses S. Grant inaugurated missionary endeavors by sending Quakers to civilize and Christianize the Plains Indians. The Quakers came to western Indian Territory, but after suffering illness and hardships of the frontier, plus getting no cooperation from the Indians, the Quakers returned home. The Episcopalians followed.

Baptist Missionary Rev. Robert Hamilton, baptizing Chief White Eagle (Blackburn) in Kingfisher Creek. Fred S. Barde Collection. Courtesy, Research Division of the Oklahoma Historical Society

The Reverend John Bartlett Wicks, an Episcopalian priest from New York, rescued David Pendleton Oakerhater (Medicine Maker), who was a Cheyenne Indian, and three other Plains Indians from the U.S. military prison in Pensacola, Florida, and took them to New York for three years to educate them in Christian missionary work. Oakerhater was ordained a priest in 1881 and then came with Wicks to Indian Territory to establish an Episcopalian mission at the Darlington Indian Agency in Blaine County,

Oklahoma. Oakerhater was one of twenty-eight Plains warriors who had been taken prisoner by the U.S. after the north Texas battle at Adobe Walls in 1874 and imprisoned without a hearing by a court of justice. Oakerhater was ordained in 1881 and served as a priest for his fellow tribesmen at the Whirlwind Indian Mission until 1917. He was honored in October 2004 with the dedication of a new sanctuary for Cheyennes at Watonga, which has been named the Oakerhater Episcopal Center (Petersen: 1971: 178–180; *DO* October 10, 2004).

Lucy Hoffman, granddaughter of Kathryn and Fred Hoffman, chosen Cheyenne Princess. Photo no. 21493.4 by Steve Dodson. Courtesy, Research Division of the Oklahoma Historical Society.

The arrival of Mennonite missionaries followed the Episcopalians. The Petters in 1892 and the Kliewers in 1898 (Linscheid 1973: 21) initiated only minor changes in the Indian way of life, but Kliewer was responsible for opening the first Indian cemetery in 1899. Prior to that time Indians had been forbidden to bury their dead below the ground.

Many Cheyennes were baptized and enjoyed the sociability of the Mennonite Mission while continuing to participate in their native ceremonies. In the 1930s, Homer Hart, a Hammon Cheyenne, served as day minister and interpreter for the Mennonite Mission Church.

Indian religious philosophy was never respected or understood by most whites. Missionaries believed that conversion to Christianity and to civilization were prerequisites for living on the same continent with Indians.

A 1910 newspaper comment (*HN* October 13, 1910) reflected the sympathetic, but condescending, attitude that prevailed toward Indians: "Not many of us are aware of the hardships endured by Rev. Kleiwer and his wife while they have labored to save the soul of the uneducated Indian."

Some Cheyenne became dissatisfied and, having retained fond memories of their experiences at the Baptist Mission and boarding school, started their own Baptist congregation in the 1940s. In 1950 Louis Littleman and Harold Flying Coyote requested support from the Oklahoma Baptist Mission board to start a Baptist Mission Church in Hammon. The request was granted. Joe Osage (WOHP-MJW September 1, 1999) detailed the planning of the new mission's beginnings:

> Services were first held under torn down trees at the camp, and eventually there was a metal—a sheet metal and tar paper shack they met in. And eventually one of the deacons from the first church, gave them some land, just over the railroad tracks from the Indian camp. And they purchased an old school building, a rural school building. They moved it on there, and that was the Indian church of the people—when they started out with 165 members. In 1959 they moved that to town, and the Baptist denomination provided the funds, and it was all built with volunteer labor.

For the next ten years the mission was placed under the sponsorship of the Hammon First Baptist Church as its "mother church," and Harold

Heiney was given the position as a full-time Baptist missionary. The mother church (the white Baptist Church) provided all of the leadership—the teachers, the officers, and the Cheyenne were designated helpers. In 1970 Max Malone, a Delaware Indian, was interviewed to be the pastor of the Baptist Indian Church and was hired.

A committee of nine members was selected to formulate a plan for the mission to become a church in its own right. The target year for separation was 1974. Nine members were appointed, one from each family in the mission. They were Nadine Orange, Bertha White Man, Elaine Bird, Inez Kauley, Inez Lone Elk, Christine Starr, Louis Littleman, Irwin Good Blanket, and Joe Osage (HIBC). The mission became a church in 1978, but the lack of money meant that it had to survive with volunteer pastors, which it did for eight or nine years.

While incorporating the notion of the Christian Jesus and God into their religious philosophy, not many Cheyennes adopted the exclusivity of Christianity. Most viewed Christianity as a way to expand and express their communion with God and the Great Spirit of the Indian religion. They also believed, as Louis Littleman commented, that:

> The whole Bible's confusing but the Cheyenne were more like the Old Testament way. When Jesus picked his twelve disciples, those were the twelve tribes. Denominations don't matter. They just don't make any difference. There's just one God and one church. It's the same God that the Baptist talks about and the Indian talks about. The Baptist Church is just another place the Indian goes to talk to God. It's his God just like it's the white man's. The laws of the Cheyenne are similar to the Ten Commandments and they [the Cheyenne] had them long before the white man came.

From 1969 onward, autonomy of leadership and policy making became a major goal of the members of the Hammon Baptist Mission, in their attempt to become independent of the mother church. The threat of no more financial support from the mother church, if certain policies were not followed, was especially upsetting to the mission members, and the withdrawal of this support, though quite meager, was greatly feared.

Mary Antelope Skin Yellow Hawk, wife of Chief Fred Yellow Hawk at the American Indian Exposition in Anadarko, Oklahoma c. 1948. Photo by Pierre Tartoue', Courtesy Research Division of the Oklahoma Historical Society.

Attendance at the Baptist Mission and the Mennonite Church in 1975 proved to be very erratic and depended a great deal on how well the current minister was liked and other considerations, e.g. Where are the best refreshments? Or, Where is everyone else going?

Joe Osage, who was a deacon in the Baptist Mission Church, volunteered to keep the doors open, but attendance was already declining. Fewer people were attending church. By 1999 only about thirty-five women were coming regularly. The doors to the church were still open in 2005, but there were no regular services. Current research shows that Plains Indians, and Plains Apaches in particular, who identify themselves as Christians, do not necessarily show a preference for one denomination over another, nor do all of them accept the exclusivity of Christianity (Parker 1986; Schweinfurth 2002).

According to Pastor Max Malone, Cheyenne attendance at the Baptist Mission ranged from ten to fifteen in the summer to about thirty-five in the winter, although official membership totaled seventy-five. Attendance at the Mennonite church services in Hammon was even smaller. The Baptist church was more successful at that time with the Indian community because the pastor, Max Malone, a Delaware Indian, was especially effective in ministering to the Indian community. Persons in the white community were not comfortable with Max's braided hair, or "the way they carry on" over there, but at the same time, more than one expressed relief that "they [the Indians] don't come to our church."

In the late nineteenth century, as Christian missionaries were having limited success in changing Indian religious and cultural values, a messianic religious movement promising supernatural deliverance was sweeping the Plains area. This took form in the resurgence of the Ghost Dance during 1889 and 1890 and was led by a young Paiute, Wovoka, who promised destruction of the white man, a return of the buffalo and old tribal ways, and a millennium in which the Indian dead would return and all would be free from misery, death, and disease.

The Ghost Dance ceremony, which spread to the Plains tribes, became a hysterical, militant, religious movement, in which participants danced all night to induce a trancelike state. They believed that the white ghost shirts they were wearing were impervious to bullets. When put to the test, however, the shirts failed, sparking the infamous massacre of three hundred Sioux, who were wearing the shirts at Wounded Knee in 1890. When the shirts failed, the movement ended.

For three decades after the massacre, at least, there were minor sporadic attempts to revive the Ghost Dance in a more subdued form. Wovoka remained a sought-after prophet who traveled from tribe to tribe healing and promising salvation. Some living Cheyenne still remember his arrival in Hammon in 1916 (*HA* March 2, 1916), at a time when the tribe's very survival and way of life were threatened by an especially high incidence of tuberculosis. The Cheyenne turned out in large numbers to get help from Wovoka, having great faith in his ability to cure the "hemorrhage of the lungs," or tuberculosis.

The Ghost Dance fostered close contact between the tribes, a mutual antagonism against whites, and a unanimity of Indians across tribal lines. During this state of heightened pan-Indian awareness, a new movement, also religious in character, arose and diffused rapidly across the Plains. It was the Peyote religion that was destined to become the most significant and widespread pan-Indian religion of the twentieth century (Stewart 1974: 211–223).

The Peyote religion, a unique blending of native religion and Christianity, provided an important cultural integrative mechanism as the Ghost Dance faded, tribal religions were prohibited, and Christianity was, for the most part, incomprehensible and irrelevant. The Peyote religion adopted the basic tenets of Christian ethics and superimposed them on traditional Indian values. It touted peyote as a sacrament.

Peyote, botanically *Lophophorus williamssii*, has a pharmacologically soporific effect that produces a euphoria and a corresponding reduction of pain in the user's body. Commonly synaesthesis—the phenomenon of stimulating the receptors of one sense to be interpreted by terms of another sense occurs. Sounds become colors and colors sounds. Peyote has a dual efficacy, revelation and healing. By producing revelatory visions, it provides communion with God and nature. By reducing pain it is important in treating physical and mental ailments (Bittle 1954).

Members organized the religion under the name, Native American Church in 1918 in the state of Oklahoma to invoke their right to freedom of religion and the use of peyote as a holy sacrament.

The power of peyote is explained by Fred Hoffman, a priest in the Native American Church: "Indians lived on herbs before the white man came. In this country of ours we did not know the Bible, God. But certain powers are in the herb that we understand. There are certain cases that the doctors have given up on. We have seen miracles performed. Those carried in would get up and walk out."

Anna Hawk's favorite story is about how peyote helped her father's crippling rheumatism:

> It was so bad he couldn't get up. Three medicine men came to him with their peyote. All night they made tea with the peyote and drank it. Then he looked up, and he saw this man come in with a black suit, forked toes, and a long tail. The other men couldn't see him, just my father. This man had a big spear and he stabbed my father in the hip. My father jumped up. The man disappeared and everyone was surprised to see him standing up. I don't know about the use of peyote for everyone. Not everybody uses it that way. Some of these men like to use it to be proud. They like to get drunk and feel proud. But that's not what peyote should be used for. It's supposed to be used as a medicine.

Probably one of peyote's most potent appeals is its capacity to help cure alcoholism, thereby contributing positively to the physical and social health of the Indian community. Many of the older Cheyennes recall episodes of how their parents advocated participation in the Native American Church hoping to curb the spread of alcoholism in the younger generation.

Fred Hoffman recalled that his parents dressed him in buckskin for his first peyote meeting at the age of five so that he would grow up to be a serious young Indian man. His father was a priest in the Native American Church, and he conducted weekly peyote meetings in the ceremonial tepee on the family allotment. Fred, throughout his childhood and youth, attended many meetings, but he ignored the church's strong prohibition on liquor even though partaking of peyote and alcohol at the same time made him violently ill. He did not take the precepts of the church seriously until many years later when he reached his middle forties.

When a person wished to take a personal vow or be healed, a special ceremonial tepee would be erected. Peyote services were held on Saturday nights. Communicants gathered around a crescent-shaped earthen mound that held the sacrament, peyote, and they smoked the sacred pipe, sang songs, and chewed peyote at the all-night ritual around the sacred fire. Fred Hoffman, in describing the religion, said, "It's a religion of free will and help. We sit on Mother Earth and pray to God."

According to Pastor Max Malone, "Hammon is known as the Vatican of the Native American Church because it is one of the strongest areas in the state for the religion. Missionaries go out from the Hammon church and preach not only to other Cheyenne groups, but to members of other tribes as well."

Estimating the number of communicants in the Native American Church is impossible because if a person attends one meeting at any time, at any age, he or she may be counted as a member. The number of communicants varies at the weekly services, but almost every Cheyenne has attended at least one peyote meeting, that is, except for the few Cheyenne who are strong in "the medicine way," and are loyal to the native religion.

Martha Fingernail explained that, when possible, family members of a deceased person plan a pilgrimage to gather peyote in honor of the deceased. She and other members of the family traveled in a car caravan to the Mexican border to search for peyote to honor Bruce, one of her favorite grandchildren. Martha recalled, "After we got there, we looked and looked and couldn't find any. It was hot. We went across the border and looked all day. But the Navajos had all of it, and they were sellin' it, but it was high and we didn't buy it. Bruce [the deceased] had always wanted to go down there. That was his dream. We felt like we were doin' it for him. That's really why we went."

The earlier, traditional forms of native religion and the Peyote religion, although weakened in today's community, are often called upon as reinforcements, when needed. In today's community the majority of rituals and beliefs have become variously synchronized. Most Cheyennes in Hammon are members of a Christian church, while rejecting the exclusivity of Christianity, and the Native American Church. Their attendance is usually sporadic, but seldom nonexistent. They also celebrate their native religion by participating in the Arrow Ceremony and the Sun Dance every summer, although the ceremonies are becoming more secular. With an all-embracing view of what God and religion should be, their religion is very pragmatic. Their preference for syncretic manifestations of religion is a viable way for them to retain their distinctive culture while accommodating themselves to an alien, industrialized America.

Chapter Eleven

"IT'S A WHITE MAN'S SCHOOL"

I learned to garden and cook, like a white man. And when I asked my father if I could go to college, he said, "No, because none of the Indian girls are learning anything at school that they can ever use. It's a white man's school." And not gettin' educated is why I ended up here [in Hammon].

--Anna Hawk

Anna Hawk bemoaned the fact that she never had the opportunity to go to school and learn a skill. She knew that there was some connection between her lack of education and the cycle of poverty in which her family was trapped. She also understood that her grandchildren could never break out of that cycle of poverty without a proper education. She believed that an education was essential for them to be independent and gainfully employed when they reached adulthood.

Early education has often been regarded as the key to desirable economic advancement for Indians as well as whites, because it involves the segment of the population that is most easily malleable, its children. If, it is argued, Indian children can learn values and useful skills to successfully live in a white world, then the Indian poverty problem can be solved. However, only the schooling considered to be proper by whites can accomplish this task.

The failure of Indian educational curricula, formulated by whites throughout the century, is glaringly evident today in the totally unskilled population, not because government funds have been lacking, but because motivation has been missing and being educated has not been highly valued by many in the Cheyenne community. There is now, however, a growing recognition that in order for young people to become independent financially someday and be in control of their own lives, they must not only have a high school education, but a college education or training in a technological skill as well.

Max Malone spoke admiringly of a local Cheyenne woman who "left the community, got a college degree, and came back to teach in the public school," a line of action believed by the white community to be an ideal situation for her, the community, and the school. But prejudice on both sides surfaced, and Pastor Malone who lamented failure of the plan, said, "It was hard for her, for the Indians said that she didn't belong to them, and the whites said that she didn't belong to them. The educated Cheyenne can't keep old friends and they can't make new ones." The woman, Dr. Henrietta Whiteman left the Hammon community, returned to school, and earned a masters degree and a doctorate from the University of New Mexico. She then became a professor of Indian Studies at the University of Montana.

Although the government had many failures in Indian policy, they did have some success in education. Chief White Shield and Chief Red Moon agreed to send their children to school if the government would build the school near their allotments. The government agreed, and construction on the Red Moon School that began in 1894 was completed in 1896 (Hodge 1978). The principal emphasis of the curriculum was the development of vocational and practical skills, but academic courses were also regarded as important. Parents balked, however, at sending their children to the school when they perceived that the main purpose of the school was to convert Indians to the white man's way. In 1899 the Indian agent at Darlington threatened to withhold annuity payments to Indians who failed to put their children in school. The result was that for each of the next four years, approximately fifty students enrolled (RCIA 1899–1902).

Southern Plains Federation of Indian Home Extension Clubs, Dress rehearsal, for women wearing street dresses they had made. Photo, Courtesy Research Division of the Oklahoma Historical Society.

Cheyenne woman in Clinton, Oklahoma, with travois that carried goods to the next location. Before the horse came to America and was available to the Cheyenne, the travois was pulled by dogs. Author's Photo

In early allotment days Indian children were required to go to private boarding schools where they could be taught white values by white administrators and teachers. Of twenty-nine Indian schools in Indian Territory, the present state of Oklahoma, three were attended by Hammon Cheyennes: the Chilocco Indian School, north of the present-day Newkirk, Oklahoma; the Mennonite Mission School in Cantonment, Oklahoma; and the Red Moon School in Hammon run by the U.S. government. There were also two government schools outside of Oklahoma: the Carlisle School, which later became Carlisle Indian Industrial School in Pennsylvania; and Haskell Institute in Lawrence, Kansas (Berthrong 1976:140–147). Most students attended from one to three years, but soon student enrollments began to decline and closures followed.

Another dimension of the private school mandate is a story told by Chief Kias about Indian recruitment at Darlington in 1874. After the married and unmarried men, old men, boys, and married women enrolled, there was a group of girls who feared that they would be sent away to school like the boys. So they sent out the word that they were ready to get married because a marriage status would exempt them from having to go away to school. Within a short time all the marriageable girls got married except one, Path, a daughter of Chief Heap-of-Birds. (*WR*, December 26, 2001).

Women had the responsibility for putting up the tepee when the tribe moved to a new location. The two sides are placed around the poles to meet at the door, that faces east. The photo is looking north. Phillips Collection. Courtesy of the Western History Collections, University of Oklahoma Libraries

Each family had a quota of sons and daughters that they were required to send to school. Parents refused to give up the children whom they loved the most, and for that reason, Chief Kias' father refused to let him go. Kias was nine years old at the time, and he, unlike the others, wanted to go to school.

At the Red Moon School, the first task was the teaching of the English language. Success came quickly, and the superintendent happily reported in 1900 that students who had scarcely "responded with a grunt" a year earlier, "were now speaking English everywhere."

The girls in the school were taught to knit stockings instead of bead moccasins, to sew, and to cook, and boys learned how to raise poultry, hogs, and cows. Crops cultivated by the students included 40 acres of oats, 35 acres of kafir corn and maize, and 50 acres of alfalfa. Each boy had an individual garden during the time that the Red Moon School was open, but the gardens were not very successful (RCIA 1900: 330). Academic courses from English to math and physics were required for all Indian students along with industrial training.

The Red Moon School complex was a structural assortment of unimaginable variety required for the far-reaching curriculum. These structures included a blacksmith shop; a food issue station, used as instructors' quarters; tent houses for students; a shed for tubercular patients; a barn used for shelter for school and agency teams and vehicles; a commissary used for storing school supplies; a laundry; a bake shop; lavatories used for school and agency; a machine shed; a coal house; a chicken house; a cow shed; a pig house; a corn crib; and a hay and stock shed for horses (ECDN, April 18, 1976).

William Smith was the first superintendent, a position he held until 1899. John Whitwell, who followed, transformed the institution into the most modern institution in western Oklahoma (ECDN April 13, 1975). Under his direction the Indian students planted hundreds of shade trees, a fruit orchard and built a number of fences. The students were speaking English in the school room as well as on the playground and making educational advances.

In 1910 the school hired Dr. Lee Dorroh to be the school's physician, a position he held until 1921. Eighty years after Dorroh left the school, in 2004, his two daughters willed the bulk of their personal estates to the Oklahoma Medical Research Foundation in Oklahoma City in memory of their father's eleven-year service at the Red Moon School (*Findings*, 2004).

In 1912 fire destroyed the hay barn and four hundred bales of alfalfa hay that had been stored for the winter at the school. In the summer of that same year two very destructive tornados hit the area and led the director of the school to request funds for a cyclone shelter, or to use the native term, "fraid hole." The money was furnished and the shelter built to accommodate students, employees, and anyone else located near the school that needed shelter (*ECDN* April 17, 1975).

At the end of the school year, when the majority of the Indian community attended Red Moon's closing exercises, local white leaders used the opportunity to lecture all Indians about better methods of farming (*HA* 1915). Anna Hawk chuckled, "They didn't care what kind of food we could get or liked. They said we needed to eat white man's food. They kinda acted like we were all retarded."

During the same period the 4-H extension services were conducting classes to teach all of the Cheyenne women and their daughters domestic skills. High on the list was sewing. Indian women learned to make dresses that looked like white women's dresses, and then modeled them in a style show. Very young girls were taught to sew handkerchiefs and scarves. Women also were taught cooking skills, how to preserve foods by canning, and how to refinish furniture that few of them had. These classes were open for all the Indian women in the southern Plains area. Transportation to the classes was furnished, and day care was available for the children too young to attend the classes.

School enrollment figures at the Red Moon School were never very stable. By 1912 the school was no longer a boarding school but was operating as a day school. Enrollment continued to decline, and in December 1915 only twenty-eight students were enrolled. By 1917, as the worldwide flu epidemic struck, killing as many as fifty per cent of the tribe, enrollment at the school dropped to fourteen. The causes were many. Sometimes the parents needed the child to help at home, especially as the highly contagious flu spread to the camping area where the parents of most students lived. Or the child got terribly homesick at the school. Some students began attending one of the many rural white schools nearer to their homes and others dropped out of school permanently. To compound the problem, students were often accompanied by their parents who camped near the school. A frequent complaint of school officials was that parents interfered with teaching. Government officials complained that the parents were neglecting their own homes and livestock in order to camp near the school to be near their children (RCIA 1905–1917).

As enrollment continued to decline, a protest was filed by the parents, requesting that the school be continued as a day school for their children, but the declining enrollment and lack of funding finally forced the school's closing on July 14, 1925 (RCIA 1925). All Cheyenne students in the school transferred to the Hammon Public School or one of the rural schools located near their family's allotment. On December 28, 1965, fire of unknown origin destroyed the Red Moon School buildings.

Although an Indian boarding school away from Hammon had always been an option for Indian children, it became particularly popular after the Red Moon School was closed. Fred Hoffman remembered that his parents wanted him to attend the local white school because they believed that white association was a definite advantage, but he experienced so much prejudice in the public school that he wanted to go back to an Indian school. With a great deal of reluctance, his parents finally agreed to let him go to the Indian boarding school in Chilocco, Kansas.

From 1925 to 1974, all Indian and white children attended the same public school in Hammon. After the Red Moon School was closed, Indian students constituted from 30 to 40 percent of the Hammon Public School enrollment each year. The drop-out rate for Indians has always been extremely high. As late as 1972, it was 67 percent (Cheyenne and Arapaho Report 1973). In recent years that figure has improved so that the dropout rate has declined to slightly above 25 percent. The reasons are multi-faceted, but the two most frequently given by Indians are: (1) cultural differences and (2) prejudice and discrimination.

Martin Fingernail said that he was not aware of prejudice against Indians until he went to school, "I didn't know I was Indian until I went to school—really high school. The discrimination was terrible. I was in fights every day. They'd call me Gut-Eater and everything else. The teacher, she called me a liar—a damned liar. I told her if I was a liar, she was a liar. And I walked out of that school and I never went back. I joined the Army and left."

Strong anti-Indian feelings have always pervaded the white community, and on occasion, parents and students of one faction or the other would boycott classes. In April 1969 a school ground fight broke out between two eighth-grade girls, one Indian and the other white. The Indians charged that the father of the white girl interceded and "choked" the Indian girl (DO April 1, 1969). Conditions exploded again in 1973 as the result of an incident at the Hammon Public School, an incident that had far-reaching consequences in the community because it not only increased tension between Indians and whites, but it inflamed old disagreements within the Cheyenne community.

On January 31, 1973, a teachers' aide, slapped Linda Zotigh, a partially deaf and blind Indian child, sparking an open confrontation between Indians and whites. Indians boycotted the schools. National AIM (American Indian Movement) and NIYC (National Indian Youth Commission) leaders arrived in town, and the local sheriff's office reinforced itself with Highway Patrol units. "The initial incident quickly grew into general charges of widespread discrimination," said Don Noconie, representing AIM. Emma Lou Standing Water Hart, chairman of the Cheyenne parents' group, presented a petition to the state's Human Rights Commission alleging, "The discrimination against Indian people in Hammon is a statewide scandal" (OJ February 20, 1973.)

Eldon Payne, the school superintendent, said that the slapping was effective and declined to reprimand the teacher. He said that the slapping on the shoulder resulted from the girl failing to do work assigned to her and noted that after the incident the girl began turning her work in on time.

Many Indians were afraid. Anna Hawk said she would always remember how frightened she was: "They said they were going to burn down other people's homes if they didn't join AIM. They had long hair, dirty jeans. They said, 'We're all Indians and we won't burn down anybody's house.' But I wanted to find out. They said, 'Why would we threaten to burn Indian houses? We want to help Indians.' But that long hair—you should have seen it".

Approximately two-thirds of the Indian students and parents did not support the 1973 boycott. Anna Hawk expressed her version of the incident: "An Indian girl said that the teacher slapped her. All the teacher did was pat her on the shoulder gently, and the girl went home and said that the teacher had slapped her. They rushed the girl to the hospital. She had always had ear trouble, but she said that the teacher had slapped her so hard that it ruined her ear. And the teacher said that she didn't know what happened. She said, 'I like these Indians. I don't have anything against Indians.'" The families who supported the boycott decided to start their own "freedom school" in the Cheyenne–Arapaho community building. One year later the school opened under the name Institute of the Southern Plains, with an enrollment of forty-two students (*DO* June 23, 1974). Strong feelings against the freedom school persisted within the Indian community for a long time. A number of Indians believed that the school did not have any required academic standards and only took the students no one else wanted. Anna Hawk, speaking for many of the traditional segment of the Indian population, expressed their skepticism:

> That school said that they had three graduate. I don't know how. Sometimes those kids got up at noon and went to school. Most of the time, they didn't go at all, and they all got diplomas. The public school is a good school. There never was any question about which school my grandchildren would go to. I send my grandchildren to the public school because it's a good school. At the AIM school, the teachers don't have any training. The AIMs got their education in the pen. They said that everybody at the new school was going to talk Cheyenne, but they lie. Nobody

speaks Cheyenne any more but the older people. Those children just go over there and draw. All those that went over there just want to be AIMs.

And for that reason she turned down $20 a day to teach the Cheyenne language at the school. She said proudly, "I wouldn't a done it for $100 a day." Louis Littleman expressed the same sentiment in different words:

> It was almost a Revolutionary War. And it was about money. Any way they came here. Those people wanted to run everybody out of town. We weren't scared. They finally got it straightened out. They rented a little building out here. They call it the Institute of Plains Indians. They had three boys graduate. How did they graduate? They don't have no superintendent. They don't have no professor. These two women went to the tribe and asked for thirty acres. All that school is, is a grade school. I don't know where they got that money.

Cootsie interrupted with, "I heard that this man, this money, this man in East Germany sent the money. It's communism." Louis agreed, "It's communism."

Peggy Dycus, a Sac and Fox Indian, was in charge at the new school. She was extremely optimistic about what the school could accomplish in spite of the fact that not everyone in town really wanted her there. It took two months for her to get a telephone and that happened because she went higher up the corporate ladder with her request to a district manager. She had been labeled an AIM, and she could not find a house to rent. She had been promised a particular house if she would clean and paint it. After a month of painting and working on the house, the owner found out who she was and rented it to someone else.

The Hammon Public School was under pressure to keep its enrollment up because if it fell below a certain number, it would be a prime candidate for consolidation with another surrounding school, so it was very important for the public school to get the Indian children back.

Eldon Payne, the public school superintendent, said, "Any Indian can come to my school with braids, with his bow and arrow—whatever he wanted."

The Institute of the Southern Plains School graduated three students—Larry Howling Buffalo, Denny Ray Standing Water, and Eugene Hart. Each was presented a white Pendleton blanket and a diploma. Peggy Dycus (*ECDN* June 24, 1974), director of the school, explained,

> The blankets are highly valued among Indians because that is one gift that will have meaning and usefulness for the rest of their lives. This commencement exercise represents another first in Oklahoma, an opportunity for Indian students to learn in school the language that their parents and grandparents speak at home. The teachers at the school, most of whom are Cheyenne, speak the Cheyenne language. All the students are Cheyenne.

Cheyennes value a Pendleton blanket highly because it is the gift item of choice that is given to honor someone or to celebrate a special occasion at a tribal or inter-tribal powwow.

Indian parents had many persistent grievances against the Hammon Public School that caused ongoing problems in Indian education—the mistreatment of Indian students, no program in the school curriculum to preserve and enrich Indian culture, the school's unwillingness to hire Indian teachers, no Indians represented on the school board to redress Indian wrongs, and alleged abuse of Johnson O'Malley government funds. The U.S. government gives JOM funds that are designated for two purposes: (1) Indian students' school needs, and (2) salaries of teacher aides who are Indian.

While most Indian students would not admit that they were mistreated at the school, many reported being stifled and humiliated. A teacher who feels justified can easily show favoritism for white children in subtle ways. One of the Indian girls in 1973 told her mother that all the white children had to have help with the speeches they were preparing for the speech contest but not the Indian children. And, later when the winners were announced, only white children won.

Many Indian students have a difficult time being motivated to attend school when they perceive that they are being treated like second-class citizens. But more important, discrimination at school makes them considerably more vulnerable to feelings of depression, and to drugs and alcohol. Anna Hawk and Martha Fingernail, among others, felt helpless to do any thing about it. Anna, obviously distressed, expressed the futility of talking to the Hammon public school officials: "It's not easy. It's hard for a grandmother to raise grandchildren here because there's so much drinkin' here. They won't stay in school, and the superintendent, he don't care. I worry all the time about Mary who is fourteen. She hasn't been to school for two days. When I asked her where she had been the day before, she just left and went over to that girl's house and didn't come home all night."

Anna walked to the grocery store every day that school was in session to ask a clerk to call the school to find out if her granddaughter was in school. If not, then Anna searched for her. When found, the granddaughter usually, but not always, refused to return to school.

Whites did not believe that the public school was a place to teach Indian heritage and culture. Eldon Payne, the school superintendent said, "The Indian should look to his home to preserve his heritage, not the school. The Indians are going to have to realize that they are going to have to conform to the ways of the dominant society. They're not Indians. They're Americans."

Indian teachers at the school promote feelings of positive identification for Indian students, but qualified Indian teachers were in short supply and the white school board seemed to have a strong bias against hiring them as teachers. "The biggest problem the Indians have here," said one Indian man, "is jealousy—things, positions, tribal jealousy, family jealousy. Everybody makes a big deal out of nothing." Several Indians from other tribes taught for brief periods at the Hammon school, but their presence did not help the local Indian situation much. Several Indian teacher aides held positions at the school that were funded by

JOM, but if the superintendent failed to apply for funds, which happened from time to time, those positions were not filled.

The use of Johnson O'Malley funds has been controversial since they became available for the Cheyenne in 1970 when the federal government transferred the administration and responsibility for the funds to the states and tribal corporations. In Hammon, a JOM committee composed of Indians was formed to make recommendations. The committee decided to hire an Indian art teacher, but because it was late in the year, a white art teacher who happened to be available was hired temporarily. Seven years later the white teacher could not be replaced because he had tenure. JOM funds were paying one-third of his salary, one-half of the nurse's salary, and one Indian teachers' aide's salary.

Johnson O'Malley funds are required to be spent on two needs: supplemental faculty, and individual expenses of Indian students. JOM pays for small, but essential costs, such as eyeglasses, shoes, school supplies, jackets for sports, band uniforms, and graduation gown rental. This money is so essential to many families, especially those with four or more children to educate, that without it some of those children could not attend school. When the committee insisted that the funds only be used for two aides, the superintendent strongly objected on the grounds that the plan would jeopardize the school's financial stability, and severe repercussions would result. So the committee relented. The day before the school term began in September of 1977, the committee discovered that the superintendent had not applied for funds because it required too much bookwork. One of the Indian teacher aides, Joyce Bull Coming, who had four children to support, lost her job. She, however, would not blame the superintendent. She said, "He's a good man. It's not his fault, but I need a job bad because I get more than I do from welfare."

On expenditures of Johnson O'Malley funds for Indian students, Eldon Payne took a strong stand:

> Since we are not on a reservation, the white children have
> a right to benefit from these funds because we don't have
> segregation in our schools. The non-Indian is discriminated
> against. What we do for the Indian child we can't do for

the others. They [Indians] get their eyes checked, they get eyeglasses, they get their teeth checked, they get their books, they get their class dues. It's all free. Everything's free. Then there's parental costs. That's clothing. The parents can take them down to Elk City and buy them shoes, clothes, anything that's parental costs. It's all free. Everything is free. The thing they've got to realize is that they're going to have to compete. They're going to have to conform to the dominant society.

In the year 2005 the executive branch of the U.S. government cut funding of Johnson O'Malley by fifty percent. For the year 2006 President Bush had recommended a cut of one hundred percent. The government alleged that Title VII made JOM unnecessary. The Cheyenne pointed out that Title VII was mostly spent on administrative costs, and that individual children would be put at a serious disadvantage if JOM funds were cut off. A letter campaign was directed to Oklahoma Congressmen from the parents of the students who would be effected. The campaign paid off, and Congress voted to keep the program.

Indians strongly believe that they have a right to these funds and that the funds should be used exclusively for programs in which white children do not participate. Others felt differently. One white person said, "Who do they have who is qualified to be on the school board? After all, you have to be educated to run, and none of them know anything about schools. Not only that, none of them have ever filed to run."

When school board vacancies occur, Indians are hesitant to file for the position. On Election Day, almost no Indians vote because very few are registered to vote. An Indian observer said, "Indians can't get organized enough to put a candidate up for the school board and support him. Many are so jealous of each other that they could never give an Indian one-hundred percent support and would probably vote for a white if they did not like the Indian."

One of the few male Indians employed in the community of Hammon in 1974 was fired when it was discovered that he supported the Indian boycott of the public school system. Those who participated in the boycott and attended the new school, or had children who attended the school, could not find employment, not even day work in the summer. A typical white attitude expressed more than once was, "Serves 'em right. Ray learned his lesson. He went back to the public school with his kids, but it takes people a long time to forget, and I don't blame 'em. Maybe some day he can get a job, and he was a good worker, too."

In spite of the gloomy picture of Cheyenne education in the past, today's Cheyenne children are faring somewhat better, but they have not caught up yet with the white children. According to the CPI or Cumulative Promotion Index, Indian students from Oklahoma, a state that has the second highest percentage of Indians in America, outperformed the nation (indianz.com February 7, 2004) in graduation rates. The picture is brighter for those who wish to become more "Cheyenne." They can immerse themselves in their Cheyenne heritage and learn to speak the language. Lenora Hart, a granddaughter of Cornstalk and John Peak Hart, and sister of Lawrence, was hired by the Cheyenne Cultural Center to finish the Cheyenne language orthography after she retired. The orthography had been started at Southwestern Oklahoma State University earlier, but it needed to be finished. Lenora also was asked to teach the Cheyenne language to undergraduates at the same university in Weatherford, Oklahoma.

In Hammon the school situation was difficult long before Eldon Payne declared: "The biggest problem we have here is the welfare system and the BIA. They've destroyed our Indian. I've seen somebody come out of the rehabilitation program and be put to work, and then a caseworker will come along and say, 'Hey, if you don't quit, you won't get your check.' So, they just quit. How's that for help? You tell me what the federal government is doing. They've just messed everybody up."

In 2006, the school was faring better than it had thirty years earlier as evidenced by an increased number of Indian students graduating. In the past it was common practice to hand out attendance certificates instead of unearned diplomas to Indian students at graduation ceremonies. Joe Osage recalled that in his seventh grade school class there were five or six Indians, but at the graduation ceremony five years later there were only two of the original group left, and only one, Joe Osage, received a high school diploma. The other Indian who shared the podium with him got an attendance certificate instead.

When I asked Lawrence Hart if he thought that the extreme school prejudice had improved, he answered in the positive. He said he believed "that the success of the school girl's basketball team seemed to have helped a lot." The Hammon Lady Warriors basketball team was undefeated in 2006. They won twenty-six games to take the state Class B title. There were four Indian girls on the team, one of whom was the top scorer, Tiffany Bull Coming. She scored twenty-three of the thirty-nine points scored by her team. A new respect from the entire student body seemed to have developed. Added to the fact that eight Indian students were graduating from Hammon High School and one was being honored as class salutatorian gave the entire Cheyenne community a real sense of pride.

Red Moon School, a boarding school that opened in 1895 for the Hammon Cheyenne. It closed in 1925 for lack of attendance. It was destroyed by fire of unknown origin in December 1965. Photo Courtesy of Patt Hodge

Victory 4-H Club Indian Girls who were ages eight to ten years of age wearing head scarves and carrying handkerchiefs they had made in sewing classes. Photo by Robert H. Wood, Robert H. Wood Collection, Courtesy, Research Division of the Oklahoma Historical Society.

Hammon teen age girls at the 4-H Club members at Chilocco Indian School for annual Achievement Day program. L. to R. 1. Minnie Yellow Eagle, 2. Cynthia Whiteskunk, 3. Carol Fingernail, 4. Irene Hayes. Teen age girls from Hammon, Oklahoma. Photo, 1954. Robert H. Wood Collection, a Research Division of the Oklahoma Historical Society

Children in Hammon play together while their mothers attend extension courses in homemaking skills. Photo 1954. Robert Wood Collection, Research Division of the Oklahoma Historical Society.

Part Four

Matrifocality

Chapter Twelve

MARRIAGE AND FAMILY: THEN AND NOW

The courtship of a Cheyenne couple during their nomadic days was a drawn-out, formal affair. Families guarded closely the behavior of their young women, who were famous for their chastity. If the couple adhered to all of the expected rules and if all parties agreed, the couple could expect to be married after a one-to-five-year courtship.

The marriage preparations began when the family of the young man who wanted to marry, sent one of its older members to approach the girl's family with the proposal, and an offer of the number of horses that his family was willing to give to seal the marriage contract. On very rare occasions a boy might skip this protocol and elope with the girl. If the girl's family consented to the marriage, an exchange of gifts between the bride's parents and the groom's parents validated the marriage.

The reciprocal aspect of marriage was an important part of the prenuptial activities, and was considered to be as important, if not more important, than the marriage. If the two families who were being united by the marriage lived in different areas, the bride's family exchanged what they had in surplus with surplus items from the groom's family. This exchange was important because it enabled tribes to acquire needed items of commodities, guns, material goods, beads, knives, and ammunition. It succeeded especially well when the families lived far apart, because there was a greater possibility that each family would have a surplus in commodities that the other family had a shortage of and vice versa (Moore 1996: 149–152).

The eldest brother living at home was the first approval authority, then the mother and father, and after them the other brothers that included her cross cousins (siblings of the opposite sex). Theoretically, the girl had no voice in the matter of the boy she would marry, but practically speaking she did because her personal feelings and welfare were strongly considered. If the young woman's eldest brother decided to betroth her elsewhere, she was expected to accept his choice. If, however, in an extreme case she chose to flout her brother's decision, it became a serious matter. Such contravention of authority created an embarrassing situation, and it affected the brother's tribal relations so severely that he sometimes contemplated suicide. In addition the girl could expect to be permanently expelled from her family.

If the young girl and her family accepted the proposal, on an agreed upon day, the prospective bride would put on her best dress, mount one of the horses the groom's family had sent, and ride to the groom's family lodge, with the person who had arranged the marriage leading the bridal horse. The bride's mother and other female members of the girl's family followed with the remaining gift horses. The bride's family added one or several horses to the gift horses and presented all of them to the groom's family, and the exchange of gifts began.

Today, courtship is of shorter duration. Family consent is not necessary, but someone in the family has to feel fairly comfortable about the decision as a practical matter, because the total lack of extra housing means that usually a newly married couple must move into a relative's home rather than one of their own. There are no new houses in the Hammon area, and new construction is not an option. So the couple moves to the house that has the most available space, if all parties are agreeable, and in many cases this is the house of grandparents.

The marriage ceremony was very simple. The bride was carried by male relatives of the groom into the tepee of the groom's family. The groom, who was also in his best clothing, extended his hand, which the bride took, and the couple were seated at a meal that the groom's mother had prepared. Sitting next to each other at the nuptial meal was the first time the couple had been together. After the meal was finished, all the relatives exchanged gifts with each other. The couple entered their new tepee that the bride's family members had erected and furnished near the tepee of the bride's parents (Ibid.).

Not all Cheyenne were born Cheyenne. Some were adopted women and children from other tribes that the Cheyenne had taken as captives and treated just like the other members of the family of the tribe. One such captive woman adopted by the Cheyennes was a Pawnee, White Horse, who was the mother of the young man who would become Chief Kias. At the age of one and a half, White Horse was sitting under a tree with her mother and grandmother in a Pawnee encampment when a Cheyenne war party attacked. The mother escaped, but the grandmother was shot and killed, and the small child was taken captive. As the little girl grew up, others told her that she was not Cheyenne, but a captive. She said she did not care—she belonged to the Cheyenne tribe. At age seventeen she had matured into a beautiful young woman and was in great demand by all of the young men. The parents of Chief War Bonnet bought her for their son to marry (WR December 26, 2001).

Unfortunately War Bonnet was one of the first Indians killed at the Sand Creek Massacre in 1864. A bullet hit White Horse in the calf of her leg, but she managed to flee Sand Creek and hide in a trench that some Cheyenne were digging. Later White Horse married Wolf-Goes-Through-the-Crowd, and they had five children, one of whom would someday become Chief Kias. After he grew up and married, Chief Kias was given a house by the Cheyenne agent, John Seger. It was the first house in Custer County (Ibid.).

Today rarely is it considered necessary to sanction the union of a couple with a marriage ceremony. If a minister is asked to marry a couple, it is for a practical reason, the most frequent one being that families cannot participate in the government's relocation program for urban employment if they have not been legally married. Six of the eight marriage ceremonies performed by the Hammon Baptist Indian pastor from 1970 to 1978 were for the relocation benefit and in all six cases the couples already had several children.

Marriages began to be less regulated by families when Indian children were sent away to boarding school starting about 1890. More possible choices for marriage partners became available outside the community, and Indian youths began to exert more independence in this area. Also, in the aftermath of virulent epidemics and intertribal hostilities in the nomadic days there was often a shortage of people, and it became common practice for a winning tribe to adopt women and children of the defeated tribe rather than keep them as prisoners. These new members of the tribe, as potential wives, were welcome, especially because they were not related. They alleviated some of Cheyenne fears about the prohibition of marrying a person too closely related. The Cheyenne had a tribal prohibition on the intermarriage of relatives, no matter how distant the relationship of the couple might be (reportedly as distant as fifteenth cousin). This prohibition was not always honored because marriages of kin did and do occur, striking fear in some of the more traditional tribal members. The fear stems from a warning in the distant past by the Cheyenne prophet, Sweet Medicine, who predicted that when Cheyennes began to marry "across the room," the tribe would die out (Powell 1969: 468).

In 1976 Martha Fingernail believed that the prophesy had already come true: "This medicine man said that when that happened, the end of the Indian world would come. It's happenin' right today. Everything this man said is comin' true." When a Cheyenne marries someone who is white or from another Indian tribe, the new spouse is automatically considered to be one of the Cheyenne community and becomes an enrolled member of the Southern Cheyenne and Southern Arapaho tribe.

Because the Hammon Cheyenne live in a small, closed community, it is extremely difficult for them to observe this prohibition. According to Martha Fingernail, after a Cheyenne married his own half-sister in the 1930s, the older members of the community believed that they were living witnesses to the doomsday prophesy. The prophesy has slowly nurtured a pervasive feeling of despair and hopelessness, especially since everybody is related to everyone else in the community to some degree.

A Cheyenne woman always had considerable status in the marriage bond in earlier days. A woman who lived in a man's lodge and had sexual relations with him automatically became a wife almost by virtue of the lack of any descriptive term, like mistress or concubine, to give her a lesser status (Llewellyn and Hoebel 1941: 81). In today's world her status is accepted and respected regardless of whether or not she was married legally, "the white man's way."

Of course, the important distinction is whether or not the couple consider themselves married. The Cheyenne mother who identifies herself as unwed when she places her child's name on tribal rolls, indirectly penalizes the future rights of that child, because even if the father of the child is a full-blood Cheyenne, the child is still listed as one-half Cheyenne. Similarly if the mother is one-half Cheyenne, her child is recorded as being one-fourth Cheyenne. As generations pass, and further dilution of Cheyenne blood occurs, a Cheyenne may find that even if he or she has the requisite amount of Cheyenne blood to qualify for tribal benefits and programs, a record of an insufficient amount of Cheyenne blood can be used to disqualify the person.

Today marriage is viewed as a voluntary union between two persons that is binding only as long as both partners desire to maintain it. It may last for a few years or for many years, and this has always been true. Today, almost everyone gets married once if not twice. Marriages contracted in the early years of childbearing generally show a greater amount of instability with the most frequent grounds for divorce being abusive treatment, incompatibility, or unfaithfulness. As couples grow older, they show a great amount of respect and affection for each other, and marriages tend to stabilize and endure. Indian–white marriages are not quite as stable. In the Hammon community there were at least thirteen Indian–white marriages from 1970 to 1977. Most of the couples over a period of time left Hammon, and five of them were divorced by 1990, according to Max Malone, the pastor of the Indian Baptist Church.

All through the nomadic, reservation, and early allotment periods a number of Cheyenne had plural wives. Usually, the wives were sisters. Whites became increasingly concerned about the practice during the reservation and allotment periods. Indian agents and missionaries finally succeeded on March 12, 1897 in pushing the territorial legislature to pass a statute prohibiting the contracting of any more plural marriages. It required that after July 1, 1897, all men who had been allotted tracts under the Dawes Act and who had more than one wife, select one woman as their lawful wife. Failure to do so would result in bigamy charges. However, enforcement was rare, and many Indians ignored the law. Fifty Cheyenne and Arapaho who already had wives in 1897 were left alone and allowed to keep their multiple wives.

Instead the authorities targeted a few of the younger men to charge with bigamy. Several decades later, the male surrogate began to be ignored and female-headed households began to form. A woman had a choice if her husband died. She could either take charge of her household, make all decisions herself, and not worry about marrying her sister's husband who was already married to her sister. Or, she could marry her brother-in-law and remain dependent on someone else in the family.

The subject of plural wives drew this statement from Anna Hawk who recalled:

> In the early allotment years, Chief Elk River had two wives—the father. All the men had two wives in those days. My husband only had one wife, but I would like it because the wives are just like sisters. The missionaries didn't know for a long time that a lot of Cheyenne had two wives. When they found out, they want everybody to be married the white man's way, but nobody paid any attention to them. The missionaries thought everybody was living in sin, but they just had two wives.

Accurate information on which to base statistical indices of marriage and divorce is impossible to obtain because 1) very few couples get married legally, 2) unions, especially of young couples, are often brief, and 3) unions are easily dissolved. Confusion comes from the difficulty of defining a divorce. A couple may choose to get divorced formally through the courts, or one marital partner may decide to separate from the other partner by simply moving to another house. After an extended separation, the couple might decide to reunite. Or, one partner might resolve the situation by marrying someone else, in which case the former marriage has ended, at least as far as one of the partners is concerned. The decision to get divorced legally is usually based on whether or not one of the partners feels that the other one might make an issue of the separation. The only problem anyone remembers resulting from failure to use legal avenues to dissolve a marriage was one time when the children of a second wife had difficulty inheriting property.

Divorce does not create an economic hardship. In seeking divorce, a man and a woman with dependent children may not merely be escaping from what they find to be an intolerable situation, but they also may be improving their economic situation. If the father leaves, the mother becomes eligible to receive Aid to Families with Dependent Children.

The Cheyenne family of today is an interacting network of kin and non-kin living in one or several households. The network is not only composed of women who are biological relatives, but also includes those who are related by marriage and friendship. The typical Indian family closely resembles the matrifocal kindred described by Geertz (1961: 79) in Javanese society and the domestic network of inter-household cooperation that Stack (1974) describes in a Black American urban community.

Today the Cheyenne nuclear family of a single parent or parents and offspring cannot easily be isolated because it is embedded in an extended family unit and functions as part of a large domestic network. Given the adverse conditions under which the Cheyenne live, nuclear families cannot survive without help from this extensive network. In times of emotional and economic crises, the extreme importance of kin ties becomes evident. Kin are called upon to support and reinforce each other, and devise ways of self-help to avert personal disaster. The variability and extensiveness of this help blur extended family boundaries and expand the concept of family in the usual sense whether we are referring to a nuclear family or an extended family. Most individual Cheyennes began to build up ties with other kinsmen in their childhood natal homes. When they marry, those ties are not broken, but are continued and frequently multiplied so that ties extend across nuclear family boundaries and expand the concept of family to a wide domestic network. In the Indian community every family is related biologically to at least several other families, and if the distance span for calculating relatedness is wide enough, all of the Indian inhabitants will be related to each other.

This all-inclusive family that is fairly typical in today's Cheyenne community is organized on the same principles as it was in the pre-reservation and reservation periods. Then nuclear families lived in separate lodges that were located in extended family groups or camps of anywhere from fifteen to twenty-five individuals. These family groups were ideal social units to cope with the uncertainty of Plains life. Several hunters were available for each household, and in case of a large kill, there were several women to cut the animal's meat into strips to dry and preserve for future use. The women harvested berries, tubers, and vegetables when available and dried them. They dressed hides, made clothing, and prepared buffalo robes that were traded for beads, guns, and ammunition. Many were skilled in the art of ceremonial decorations that were displayed on robes and lodges, and they cared for the children.

When men were away from the camp on raids or hunting expeditions for a long period of time, women had all of the domestic responsibilities in the camp. The sharing of many of these responsibilities generated strong ties among women, especially those who were blood related. The extended family cared for the children, and divorce or death of a spouse did not break up the organization (Eggan 1955: 82–83).

It is clear that flexible domestic networks in which women have significant roles are characteristic of Black American domestic life as well as families in other ethnic groups. Whether or not these units are termed matrifocal units is a matter of choice by those doing the studies and does not alter the fact that in Hammon these Cheyenne mothers and grandmothers play a central kin role.

The responsibilities of women during the nomadic period were extensive. Women prepared all of the food for the extended family and took care of the children. They cleaned the buffalo hides to make robes that were traded for guns, blankets, beads, and ammunition. They beaded moccasins, pipe bags, and ponchos, and when the decision was made for the tribe to relocate to be nearer an improved source of water, timber, or more abundant game, or farther from the enemy, the women moved the camp. They gathered, packed, and strapped family belongings to a travois, an A-shaped carrier device fashioned from wood poles and pulled by a horse (by dogs in earlier times).

When a place to camp had been agreed upon, the women cleared the weeds and undergrowth, hung up robes or lodge skins to serve as windbreaks, built a big fire in the middle of the new camping grounds, and assumed responsibility for erecting the tepees, a task that could not be accomplished by any single individual. These cooperative tasks promoted the formation of strong bonds between women. Those who were sisters and had lived near each other all of their lives were especially close. Grinnell (1923 1:128) believed that although the women performed many laborious tasks, the work done by the men, which was mainly hunting and going to war was so important for everyone's safety, that the men had to be unencumbered when the tribe was moving in order to best repel enemies. So women were the transporters of tribal goods, pulling and carrying all of the tribe's paraphernalia to their next location.

Based on observations made in the 1920s, Grinnell (Ibid.) concluded that "among the Cheyennes, the women are the rulers of the camp. They act as a spur to the men, if they are slow in performing their duties. They are far more conservative than the men, and often hold them back from hasty, ill-advised action." Llewellyn and Hoebel (1941: 78) expressed skepticism, stating that "it is a bit of a stretch to state that women rule the camp," but conceded that "their women's position was not without power." They also said that women were strong-willed and aggressive and were by no means downtrodden. If we can conclude that there was a great deal of variance from family to family in the authority-power balance, it is likely that even though some men were very authoritarian, they, as well as the men who were not authoritarian, articulated their wives' opinions and acted upon them.

A similar authoritarian-power relationship can be found in Laos where "the strength of the adult women's local kin networks enables many women to demonstrate authority in the family and the community even though men are the formal household heads. Women mainly demonstrate this authority by controlling the labor of family members and in representing their families to the larger community. Women mainly have resources in the form of inheritance, land, labor, or allies in the case of conflict. One result of forcing residence in the wife's village is that the wife's relatives are more likely to be involved in household activities. Although a man is nearly always the household head, men's household headship is commonly tempered by the wife's kinship. Since women inherit the family home and property, they have the resources to back up the authority to act in the community" (Ireson-Doolittle 2004: 62–64).

The Cheyenne woman always occupied a position of considerable importance in the family, especially as she grew older. As a young woman with small children, she was expected to be a dutiful mother and to defer to her elders. As her family grew, she directed the activities of the extended family, and by the time she became a grandmother and acquired elder status, she was as respected as a man, and sometimes had as much power. Not only did she exercise great influence in the family, but in the tribe as well. She was often consulted by young men as well as women, because she was especially considered to possess knowledge and wisdom in sacred matters, tribal history, and herbal medicines. She was critically important in passing her expertise in the design and production of beaded materials.

In earlier times, most women belonged to at least one of several craft guilds that were composed of women who were at varying levels of beading skills. As an apprentice, a young woman was taught beading designs and patterns by an older woman.

Among today's impoverished Cheyennes, the role of grandmother has become crucially important to the viability of the family. The strong dependency that has developed between members of the kin group and its senior woman is a relationship that provides optimum stability in an indifferent world. The older woman provides support in many forms for all family members, especially the youngest. It is quite usual to find an older woman providing for the total care and education of grandchildren and forming ties with them that are stronger than ties to her own children and their mothers.

In the past, female relatives cooperated in many activities. Women often shared an outdoor fireplace and a meat-drying rack, and they worked together at tanning hides, slicing meat, and sewing skins and many other domestic chores. In some families all the food was prepared in the oldest woman's lodge and carried by her daughters to their own lodges for consumption (Eggan 1955: 61, 82–83). The son-in-law was expected to provide meat for the group kindred and even though his mother-in-law lived close by, he was expected to avoid her and definitely not speak to her (Hoebel 1960: 22).

The most common residential pattern practiced by newly wed couples was matrilocal, the post-marital residence of a bride and her new husband with or near the wife's parents. This residential pattern allowed daughters to stay close to their mothers. An exception was the patrilocality of the Dog Soldiers, a military society that became especially powerful during the middle of the nineteenth century when military activities against the U.S. Army accelerated. Matrifocal totally changed to patrifocal. The custom of a newly wed Dog Soldier and his wife was to move in with or near the parents of the husband. The increased military emphasis in Cheyenne life during the intense conflicts with the U.S. Army required a group organization that could respond quickly to attack. Patrilocality, however, began to lose its significance after the surrender.

In today's Cheyenne community, matrilocal residence is still the most common residential pattern, in part because mothers and grandmothers of young brides provide the most needed and stable source of help. The Cheyenne network of kindred has a female emphasis that is more exaggerated today than in the past. Disruptions to the social and economic life of Cheyennes during the past century have caused an amplification of duties and responsibilities of female relatives, so that women's importance vis-à-vis men's in the extended family, have increased. In the accompanying family histories there are several examples of patrilocality, the post-marital residence with or near the husbands' parents' home. When Fred Hoffman married Kathryn, Fred moved her into a lodge adjacent to his parents' lodge on the river. A few years later, he moved her to his parents' new home on the Hoffman allotment, a circumstance that can largely be attributed to the fact that the Hoffman home was where the most space was available. Through the

149

years, Vinnie and Kathryn, mother-in-law and daughter-in-law, formed a very strong bond, one that was as strong as the blood bond between mother and daughter, as with Anna Hawk and Beulah Larney, Martha Fingernail and Joyce Bull Coming, Martha Fingernail and Christine Starr, Lillie Hayes and Cootsie Littleman, and others.

The stronger bonds for women than for men can be at least partly explained by the matrilocal residential pattern, that allowed daughters to remain close to their mothers. A woman felt closer to her sister's children because they were living in the same camp as she and her children were. Bonds to her brother's children were weaker because the brother's children lived in a different camp than she did, the brother's wife's family camp (Eggan 1955: 28–29).

The Cheyenne have a bilateral kinship system meaning that kinship is equally important on the mother's side and the father's side. Cheyenne kin terms lump persons of the same gender and same generation together. They use the same kin terms for persons who have similar responsibilities and duties and different terms for those with different responsibilities and duties. A young woman speaking in the Cheyenne language referred to her children and her sister's children as, "son" (*na*) and "daughter" (*na'ts*), but she called her brother's child by a different term, "niece" (*na' ham*) and "nephew" (*nats*). She called her mother, all of her mother's sisters, and all of her mother's cousins, "mother" (*na'go*) and her father, her father's brothers, and her father's cousins, "father" (*nihu'*) (ibid: 42–49).

John Seger, in the following, reported a slight variation of the kin terminology that he had observed: "Although an Indian may be poor, he or she may have several mothers. After the real parent dies, the aunt, or aunts, take the place of the mother. It is seldom that an Indian child becomes an orphan. They regard cousins (to be) the same as brothers and sisters and distinguish them as their 'far' brother or 'new' brother. (Peery 1933: 862)."

Both parents were equally important to the children. On the parental level "mother's brother" (*naxan*) and "father's sister" (*nahan*) had special terms because they came from different kindred. Father's brother was classed with the father, and mother's sister with the mother (Eggan 1955: 42–49). The Cheyenne put an emphasis on seniority, but only in one's own generation. They distinguished "elder brother" (na'ncha) from "younger brother" (na:sima) and "elder sister" (nam han) from "younger sister" (na:sima). Younger sister and younger brother were called by the same term (na:sima), illustrating that relative age was more important than gender (ibid.).

The grandparent–grandchild bond was a very affectionate one. The terms grandfather namcim and grandmother nish'ki were extended to other older relatives by the grandchild to show respect. Grandparents were expected to spoil their grandchildren and to defend them in hostile circumstances.

Kinship terminology served to reinforce the surrogacy of several women as mothers and several men as fathers so that if the biological mother or father should die, which they frequently did in the nomadic era, the adjustment for the child would be less traumatic than it would have been otherwise. The child still would have several mothers and fathers who were not strangers.

Kinship terminology is a reflection of kindred behavior that can be very restrictive to the extent that in some relationships a policy of avoidance of each other is the rule. This is especially true with the brother–sister relationship. The brother–sister relationship is one of formal respect and restraint. There can be no physical contact or joking between them and they must not speak to each other, especially after puberty has been reached.

The son-in-law mother-in-law relationship was also one of complete avoidance. They could never speak, look at, or be in the same room with each other. But if the son-in-law performed exceptionally well in all things for a lengthy time, the mother-in-law could honor him with a Quilling Society feast in her lodge. The son-in-law would give her a lodge or a horse, and she, in turn, would give him a buffalo robe with dyed porcupine quills and present it to him at the feast. From the time of the feast forward, the incest taboo was no longer in effect (Eggan 1955: 55–56).

After World War II full employment ended, and the economic environment in the town worsened. Joblessness midst the discrimination and prejudice of the surrounding white population added to the doomsday warning from Sweet Medicine, produced a general feeling of despair. Although all who had been in the military service received government checks, the amount was inadequate to feed a family and pay the utilities. Women became more important after the war's end due to the lack of gainful employment for men and a shorter life span for men on average. The consequence of the unfriendly economic environment would guarantee for the future a largely uneducated population living in extreme poverty.

Chief Kias in front of his house near Clinton which Mr. Seger gave him after his marriage. Photo no. 15169. Kias said this was the first house in Custer County, except for log cabins. Courtesy of the Research Division of the Oklahoma Historical Society.

Chief Kias and Shell Woman, his second wife. Courtesy Betty Hart.

Chapter Thirteen

HOUSEHOLD COMPOSITION: THEN AND NOW

Characteristics of the grandmother focused family are both visible, those that can be verified by sight, and transparent, those that are unseen and discerned by the mental process. The most visible characteristic is household composition, manifest by today's presence of female-headed households, with a constant shifting of residences by children and young unmarried males and females. Transparent characteristics are those that refer to behavior and are not quickly communicated.

It was not safe in the prehistoric period for women to live alone. If a woman became a widow, the brother of her deceased husband was obligated to marry her, even if he already had a wife, a custom that was called the surrogate. Sometimes, the man married several sisters from the same extended family, which was one method of increasing numbers of people in his family and his band. The chiefs and headmen, being highly competitive, used the surrogate as a method to increase their numbers because the larger their following, the more prestige they would acquire.

Today the Cheyenne domestic network is made up of people bound together primarily by ties of kinship. Its membership fluctuates continually, not only by the birth, death, marriage, and divorce of family members, but also by the common practices of the fosterage of children and frequent visitation by friends and relatives. The composition of a household is constantly in flux. An individual may eat in one household and sleep in another. Or, that person may shift periodically between two or three households and consider himself or herself a member of one, both, or all three. It is difficult to determine who belongs to which household at any given time.

Crowding was and is severe. At any given time as many as one to six or more of the forty-five houses might be vacant. The main reason is that a number of houses were in such a dilapidated condition that the owners had to move temporarily to a relative's house until the BIA repair team could arrive to put their houses back in livable condition. Sometimes a family waited as long as several years. According to people's memories, this was a normal occurrence. The other reason a house was not inhabited was because no one, especially the more traditional Cheyenne, wanted to live in a dwelling where some relative or friend had died. It was regarded as dangerous to inhabit any dwelling that might harbor ghosts, and ghosts always liked to hang around the dead.

In prehistoric times, a family of traditional Cheyenne would abandon their tepee, tear it down, or give it away if a member of the family died in it. When a death occurred leaving a widow and children, they retained nothing. They would live with relatives for a year or two until someone supplied them with another tepee (Grinnell 1923 2:163). The decision to move out of the house today is determined by how strongly relatives feel about the traditional custom and how badly the owner needs the rental income, as well as how much space is available in a prospective relative's home.

In 2005 the Hammon–Elk City Indian community population was estimated by Joe Osage, the Indian Baptist deacon who oversees the church, to be 247 persons in Hammon proper plus the approximately twenty-five to fifty persons in the ten government houses located in Custer County. Five are on the east side of the main road going north into Hammon, and five are four miles east of those houses. Added to the 247 in town, the total Cheyenne population of Hammon is loosely estimated to be between 275 and 300.

Household composition is strongly affected by the relationship between the family and its means of subsistence. To exist as a viable domestic unit, each household must have at least one economic resource, whether from welfare, outside employment, or beadwork. To help, the BIA has a fund from which it distributes money to families who are below the poverty line or have emergency needs during the year. It is called the Emergency Assistance program, and it is operated on a first come, first served basis on "EA Day."

Beadwork, the teaching of some Cheyenne language classes at surrounding schools, and summer agricultural employment enable some families to be independent part of the time and perhaps even to help others. A little more than half of all households receive money from land leases, but because the land holdings have been so fractionalized by family inheritance, these amounts are, more often than not, quite small. Many are $18 to $20 per year, while only a few are in the upper range of $1200 per year.

With the oil boom restarting in 2002, amounts paid for oil leases rose considerably, but with another generation inheriting mineral rights, that only means that at best, for each succeeding generation, a one-fourth interest becomes an eighth, an eighth becomes a sixteenth, et cetera.

Housing occupancy arrangements, both permanent and temporary, reveal a mother focus and a grandmother focus as well. Of the thirty-nine occupied houses in the community in 1975, eighteen were headed by women, thirteen by men, and eight households had a membership that fluctuated constantly so that no determination of head of household could be made. More than half, or twenty-two of the households, were multigenerational, thirteen of which were headed by women and nine by men according to the U.S. census.

The U.S. census defines a female-headed household as a household in which the female head has no resident husband, although a son, son-in-law, brother, uncle, or perhaps an unrelated male might be living in the house. A male who does not have a regular income will be in some kind of dependent relationship with the female head. Fourteen of the thirty-nine households had regular monthly income and received from one to as many as four government checks every month from AFDC, Aid to the Blind, Aid to the Disabled, Old Age Pension, and/or regular employment. The others were dependent on irregular sources of income.

The transparent characteristics of a grandmother focused family are manifest in the unexpressed relationship of the husband and wife, as defined by R.T. Smith (1996: 54), and Bott (1968: 69). Matri-focused or mother-focused refers to the stage in family development beginning with the birth of the first child and extending to the time when the youngest child reaches the early teens. It is a time when the relationship of the husband and wife is most at risk. The bond of mother and child or children becomes stronger, and the husband–wife bond weakens. The bonds that the women in the household form are built on cooperation in everyday activities. There are sisters, mothers, and aunts. If the husband and wife have different friends and separate areas of interest and do not cross over into each other's domain, then the husband is likely to feel marginalized and seek companionship elsewhere, return to his maternal home, or spatially isolate himself in his house. This stage of the family mends itself and gradually reaches the next stage which is when all of the children are graduated or nearly graduated from high school and have married and/or left home.

Historically the grandmother focused household has been most prevalent in families that practice matrilocality (the custom of a newly married couple establishing their first residence in the bride's family encampment). If matrilocality is practiced, then the new bride will remain close to all of her relatives she has lived near all of her life. It is the husband who is the newcomer.

In the thirteen male-headed households in 1976, only one male had no wife. Of those who received regular monthly checks, approximately half were men and half were women. Eleven of these households received monthly income from Aid to the Disabled, Aid to the Blind, Old Age Pension, Veterans Administration, or regular employment. Only five men in the community were regularly employed, and they lived in the male-headed households.

Complicating the household statistics were two categories of persons who were most likely to shift residence: (1) young children who are discussed in the section on fosterage and child shifting, and (2) young and middle-aged males, both married and unmarried. A typical Hammon Cheyenne male between the ages of fifteen and forty-five often shifts residence from his home with a wife to the home of one of his maternal kin. This shifting seems to be strongly tied to economics. When a man has no job, as is frequently the case, he feels more welcome and secure among his maternal kin, as we see in the families of Anna, Martha, and Lillie. Occasionally, he will move to his mother's home with his wife or his children or all of his immediate family. In one family, one of the sons and his wife left jobs in a distant town and returned to Hammon to move in with the grandmother, and the son's mother took responsibility for the children.

Many of the female-headed households were occupied by widowed grandmothers and one or more grandchildren. Emma Lou Standing Water Hart stated the obvious: "We don't hardly have any men folks around. They're all gone." Anna Hawk lamented the Indian woman's plight in the following:

> I knew what was going to happen to my husband before it
> happened, but I had been taking care of everything anyway.
> Oh, it was hard, but that's the way it happens for Indian
> women. My father tell me a man and a woman who are
> married are going up this road, and the first thing that happens
> is the man dies and goes off on another road. The children
> have to look to the mother because she is always the one who
> is left. The Indian woman always lives longer than the man.
> Then the children go down the same road when the mother
> dies. Nobody has to have a man, because so many of us Indians
> are widows. Men are important, but when they're not around,
> the other man God is always up there for help. I know there
> are many things I cannot do as well as a man, but I have to try.
> I do the best I can. Life is hard for us Indians. Nobody knows
> how hard.

Indian women, especially the elderly, prepare themselves mentally for the eventuality of widowhood. The life span of Indian males is shorter than the life span of Indian women. The consequential disproportion of women to men tends to magnify the importance of the female role. The community had a low sex ratio (number of males per 100 females) that was 76 in 1970. Before 1900 a low sex ratio was somewhat compensated for by the practice of polygyny. Women did not live alone. Men were permitted to have several wives, and female-headed households were almost non-existent. Today a low sex ratio has quite different implications for the functioning of the family. A scarcity of males means that one can expect to find a number of households headed by women. It is important to emphasize that the disparity in the sex ratio may not be as great as the U.S. Census figures indicate because Indian men are usually under-counted. They are harder to find because some are traveling to look for work, some are on extended visits, and some deliberately absent themselves for welfare reasons (their mates cannot qualify for AFDC if the husbands are present at census time).

The actual ratio of men to women, which cannot be determined exactly, is low, which can be explained by two factors. First, in areas of high unemployment more men migrate than women. Because men do not have direct responsibilities for the care of children, they are freer to leave. Second, more men than women are victims of the hazards of life. The biodemographics of a higher injury rate and a higher illness rate for men than for women is evident in the many homes with widowed women and unemployable men.

The relationship between Cheyenne men and women has always been somewhat detached, and the romantic love that characterizes Anglo-American relationships is not readily observable in the Cheyenne. That Indians in Hammon are unemotional is not unique. Many American Indians exhibit stoicism.

Indian birth rates have historically been low, but began to increase in the early part of the twentieth century and continued increasing until they reversed in the 1970s. The decrease in birth rates in the 1970s made a significant impact on household composition almost immediately. Indian birth rates, which are affected by cultural norms began to rise at a fast pace, faster than for any other ethnic group in the U.S., and then they dropped back to slightly above cultural norms. Anna Hawk explained, "Way back when the Cheyennes had just one or two kids they always had plenty to eat. And that was nice. They waited until children could help themselves before they had more. But when they had just one or two kids, they were always having war with other tribes. They always say that people who have just one or two kids are greedy. If they have no children, they are mean and selfish. It's better to have three or four kids."

Traditionally the Cheyenne spaced their children far apart. During the period from the nomadic buffalo-hunting era to the early part of the twentieth century, the ideal time for a couple to wait before having another child was about ten years. Although some families had several children, couples who spaced their children far apart were considered to be a great credit to their tribe and were praised for their self-control. Long intervals between children allowed time for a child to complete his or her important years of training and to reach an age of some independence before parents had to divert their attention to another child. Many of the earliest historians, anthropologists, missionaries, and explorers (Llewellyn and Hoebel 1941: 169–211; Powell 1969: 446; Grinnell 1902) who spent time with the Cheyenne praised the Cheyenne women for their ability to regulate family growth.

Today, the interval between the births of children has decreased. Although some families adhere to the traditional spacing of children, many are having children only a few years apart, thereby contributing to a growing birth rate among young Indian women.

Statistics for birth rates in the town of Hammon in the year 2006 are not statistically meaningful because the sample is small. However, state and national statistics show a growing birth rate for all Indian groups. In the 1990s and the first decade of the twenty-first century, the birthrate of Indians nationwide was approximately twice that of the non-Indian population (COP 2004).

Indians place a high value on children. Programs designed by whites to limit Indian births tend to cause a reverse reaction. Indians believe that the extent to which they endorse family planning should be their decision and therefore balk at family planning imposed by outsiders. Today the whole subject is fraught with suspicion and viewed by many as a grand design by the white man to do away with the "Indian problem." Tension runs close to the surface when the Cheyenne discuss birth control. Many interpret efforts along the family planning line as an attempt to breed Indians into oblivion.

Although more children can mean more impoverishment, a higher birth rate is an obvious solution to Cheyenne survival as a people. While this conviction is openly expressed by only a few, it is nevertheless present. As parents and daughters ignore birth control information, teenage pregnancies continue. It can be argued that money available from AFDC strongly encourages the conception of children without a financially supporting father. It may, but the availability of welfare is often viewed as a safety cushion rather than a precipitating factor. It is very difficult to prove that any particular young woman is calculating AFDC payments when she allows herself to become pregnant. But certainly, the anticipated income serves as a defense when one or both of her parents criticize her condition. One young woman responded to her concerned mother, "You shouldn't care. It won't cost you nothin."

An important factor contributing to the increased birth rate is that a young woman knows that if she becomes pregnant and has a child, she does not have to assume full responsibility for the child, financially or emotionally. The care of her child will either be shared or fully assumed by her mother, grandmother, or perhaps an aunt or a sister. A belief among some traditional families is that the child belongs as much to the young woman's extended family as to herself. Child care patterns in household composition support this argument.

One mother insisted that her pregnant daughter get legally married because the mother did not want the responsibility of another child. The young couple married, the child was born, and the girl's mother assumed care of the child.

Parenting roles in today's families have changed since reservation days primarily because today the Cheyenne are part of the larger white society whereas in the earlier period they lived freely in relative isolation protected from contamination of their values by the white population. Children were not disciplined. They were taught by example.

Although traditional norms pertaining to sexual relations have changed very little since the tribal period, actual behavior has changed considerably. In earlier days unmarried girls were raised in a very strict environment and were carefully guarded during activities involving members of the opposite sex. Parental training emphasized self-restraint and voluntary self-denial (Grinnell 1923, 10: 108, 121, 156).

Today, while the older generation lectures on sexual abstinence until marriage, many adolescents begin sexual experimentation as soon as they reach puberty. Open disapproval by parents and grandparents has little impact on their behavior. As one grandmother said, "We talk to them and we tell them what is right, but they don't listen. In the camp we had some problems, but not like today. We'd tell them what was right and what was wrong, and they'd listen. We had more control down there. The bus would take them to school and bring them home. They didn't run around all the time."

The oldest generation has difficulty coming to grips with the younger generation's pursuit of personal autonomy. Guided by a traditional emphasis on sexual modesty and reticence, the older women give advice that only touches the surface of the situation. Another grandmother, shaking her head over the futility of her advice, related the following: "I told Jeanette that it was all right to let a man hold her hand, and if he tried to kiss her, then to knock him away. That kind of man's no good. He's got no respect."

❧

Beulah Larney, Annie Hawk's daughter, expressed the futility of trying to teach responsibility to her son. "He's just like Johnson grass—wild—like a weed. Maybe I should've been strict with him. Maybe my mother could have helped him. It's too late now."

David Pendleton Oakerhater (Medicine Maker), a Cheyenne who was imprisoned at Fort Marion, Florida, was rescued and trained to be a priest in the Episcopal Church. He returned to the Cheyennes as a priest in 1881 and served until 1917. Roman Nose is on the left in the picture, and the other three persons are unknown. Barney Hillerman Collection. Courtesy, Research Division of the Oklahoma Historical Society

Chapter Fourteen

FOSTERAGE AND CHILD SHIFTING

In impoverished societies beset with the daily financial unpredictabilities, such as the Cheyenne, the nuclear family needs help in caring for its children. The most frequent response to this in societies where the kin bond remains strong (E. Goody 1968; Stack 1974) has been the creation of networks of cooperating kinsmen or kinswomen who assume child care responsibilities as needs arise. Extended family responsibility is more intense in these societies than in industrialized societies where the response to deprived and unwanted children is more formalized. In the impersonal setting of the large cities, needy children are commonly adopted, institutionalized, or placed in foster care in an unrelated family home. (J. Goody 1969: 76).

The responsibilities that kinsmen assume in regard to the care of needy children are of utmost significance to the stability of the Cheyenne family. Mothers and fathers in times of crises always know that there will be a female relative who can be counted on. As the economic and social fortunes of nuclear families rise and fall, children can be passed from mothers to grandmothers, to sisters, and back to mothers.

The Cheyenne response to a needy child has been in two forms. The first is fosterage, or the rearing of another's child as one's own. For the Cheyennes it is a temporary obligation of kinsmen to take care of one another's children. Crisis situations are circumstances which most frequently initiate it and can, therefore, be called crisis fosterage, a term

165

used by Esther Goody (1973: 1992) to refer to a situation when children are fostered as a direct result of the sudden dissolution of the nuclear family unit. In the case of the death or serious illness of either parent or of divorce, the extended family cushions the resulting disruption of family life for the child. Circumstances most likely to bring about crisis fosterage are (1) when an unmarried mother is considered too young to assume full responsibility for the rearing of her child; (2) when a nuclear family unit has too many children to feed; (3) when a child becomes unruly and chronically misbehaves in his parents' home; (4) when the parents divorce or separate, and (5) when one parent dies, becomes seriously ill, or needs to move.

Being raised by grandparents is not a pattern unique to the Hammon Cheyenne. Many Indian and other ethnic grandmothers raise their children's children. If the parents are young teenagers as some are, then the maternal grandmother is likely to become the caretaker of the first child. The parents of the child are often very young and too inexperienced to know how to take care of a newborn, in the opinion of other members of the family. Fosterage is a solution of some permanence for the nuclear family's problems and needs, since the child lives in another's home for a long period of time, at least a year or more or until the crisis is over.

Each of the six families covered in this study has experienced fosterage in some form to some degree for a variety of reasons. Martha Fingernail, for example, was raised by her mother's sister and she did not know until many years later, after her children were born, that her aunt was not her biological mother.

Some times Cheyenne children moved to grandmother's house when a parent became seriously ill and the grandmother had the means and a desire to provide care for the child. As mentioned earlier, Lawrence Hart lived with his grandmother for the first six years of his life.

Martha Fingernail fostered many grandchildren in her lifetime for a variety of reasons. Her grandson, Bruce Orange, moved to her house from his mother's (Nadine's) house from where he had been living with his ten brothers and sisters. His move to Martha's house helped relieve the very crowded conditions of his large family. He was one of Martha's favorite grandchildren. He lived with her for several years, and Martha said that she felt like he was her son. She had a bed for him, she prepared his meals, but most important, she provided space for him.

Martha also fostered many other grandchildren. Among them were the three children of her daughter, Louise. Martha took care of the children until the Welfare Agency took them away and vowed to keep them until "the parents got straightened out."

Many grandchildren were also fostered by Anna Hawk. Most of the ones who moved in with her were children of one of her sons, not her daughters. Sometimes the reason for moving to grandmother Anna's house was because the parents of the grandchild were getting a divorce or separating.

In the year 2006, Emma Lou Standing Water Hart, as resident grandmother, was responsible for the primary care of five grandchildren and great-grandchildren in her house. The reasons were varied—the death of a parent, a divorce, both parents were working, loss of a job by one or both parents, or the child simply wanted to live in his grandmother's house.

Emma Lou took care of five boys, ages three, five, twelve, fifteen, and seventeen. The two oldest boys were under her care because their father had died in an accident in Montana and their mother had to go through the court system in Oklahoma to get custody of them. She never came. She remained in Montana.

Emma Lou's twelve-year old grandson did not want to go to school in Clinton where his mother was working. He wanted to go to school in Hammon and live with his grandmother. The two youngest children were sons of Lelah, Emma Lou's granddaughter, who had moved her children into Emma Lou's house. Because her grandmother was available to keep the two boys, Lelah was able to work the early morning shift at a nearby restaurant. She was divorced and had no source of income except a welfare check and what she could earn. During the day the three older children were in school, but the other two were very active children who required supervision twenty-four hours a day.

Vinnie and Kathryn Hoffman fostered grandchildren in their separate houses and sometimes the grandchildren came and stayed for many months. Those who came to Vinnie's house when she was in her eighties would stay and help her with household chores.

Another Cheyenne who lived in his grandmother's house for an extended period was Joe Osage, the son of Pete Osage and Alice Miles. Actually his mother's Cheyenne name was Alice Heap of Birds but her great grandfather many years earlier admired the agency superintendent, John D. Miles, so much that he took Miles for the family name. Joe was born in Cantonment, Oklahoma, in 1939. Both of Joe's parents died when he was ten years old, and he moved to Hammon where his grandmother and two uncles lived. He recalled living north of Hammon in Chief White Shield's camp in the 1940s (WOHP JO JA September 1, 1999).

Bonds between the grandmother and the grandchild, on the whole, became stronger than bonds between the mother and child. Lillie Hayes, a grandmother of the first generation, and her grandson, Leroy, formed a bond that was very strong. Leroy lived in her house intermittently for several years. No matter what his condition when he returned to her home, any time of day or night, she had a bed for him. She put up with his wide personality swings. She loved him and she protected him.

The second type of response to a needy child has been a more impermanent child shifting. While the duration of child shifting may be as long as that of fosterage, it also involves a rotation back and forth of a child between his or her natal home and a relative's home on a fairly frequent basis. Circumstances that bring about child shifting are the same as for fostering except that the crises are not as extended or as severe and the grandmother's love for the child is as much a precipitating factor as need. The grandmother may care for the child every weekend in the summer because she loves the child, but when probing deeper we find that some social or economic crisis is often alleviated by the transfer.

Sam Hart (WOHP-MJW May 19, 1999 an older brother of Lawrence, was born north of Hammon on his grandparents' allotment, the John Peak Heart allotment, in 1931. Sam's grandparents had moved to the allotment sometime after 1915, and in conjunction with the government, built two houses, one for themselves and one for Lawrence and his new wife, Betty. Since Sam's parents' (Homer and Jenny) house and his grandparents' (Cornstalk and John Peak) house were next to each other, it was easy to visit back and forth. Sam remembered, "There were times when I would prefer to go overnight to my grandfolks, and spend the nights and days over there. At night I could listen to my grandmother tell bedtime stories."

Children are most frequently fostered with grandparents. Because of the extremely low sex ratio in the Cheyenne community (meaning few men), the often widowed grandmother is more likely to be the foster parent. Many children are under the primary care of a grandmother, and many others are kept in a grandmother's home on a regular basis. The degree to which this is true has led many members of the white community to refer to the Cheyennes as a grandmother-oriented culture.

The grandparent–grandchild bond has always been an affectionate, indulgent one in Cheyenne society. In traditional times grandparents were expected to spoil their grandchildren. If the parents were thought to be too harsh with their children, the grandparents would threaten to bring them up themselves. The grandchild looked up to his or her grandparents, treating them with deference because of their age and knowledge. He or she was pretty much on a footing of equality with them. The grandparents were like tribal libraries. They had a wealth of knowledge about Cheyenne history, their migration route, friendly tribes, enemy tribes, and the hunt. The grandchildren especially loved the old stories and myths that had been passed down from one generation to the next and the stories of personal experiences (Eggan 1955: 53).

Grandparents did not rigidly discipline the children but neither did the parents. It was not necessary because Cheyenne children were taught by example. Today, few discipline their children or grandchildren, even if it might be necessary. Anna Hawk explained: "It's not the Cheyenne way to discipline the children. We talk to them. We tell them what is right and wrong, but we never discipline. We love our grandchildren and want them to do right, but they don't listen. In the old days the children always listened. They wanted to do right. But now they are out of control."

Martha Fingernail added, "Cheyennes are easy with their children. Whites say 'No', but Cheyennes are easy."

The most frequent cause of fostering is a divorce or a death. Sometimes a woman marrying for the second time may hesitate to take her children from her first marriage to a new marriage. She then may leave some or all of the children in the care of her mother or her mother's sister, or less frequently, with the father's mother and perhaps keep one or none with her. Sometimes, the father keeps the children of a dissolved marriage if he fears that his former wife might neglect them or he might put them in the care of his mother or sister as Freeman Hawk did. Because many divorces are not legalized with permanent custody settled in court, children might be fostered for a couple of years and returned to the mother. Who has custody of the children is an ongoing dispute in some families. As fortunes change, so do the residences of the children.

When a very young Cheyenne mother, living in the household of one or more of her parents, gives birth to a child, she frequently takes her newborn child to her grandmother's house for an extended stay. The grandmother then becomes a foster parent as she assumes primary care of her great grandchild. However, the mother may instead shift the child from her grandmother's home to her parents' home on a fairly regular basis. The child may stay for only brief periods in one home, such as weekends, or maybe for the entire summer.

Fosterage is a matter of personal choice as well as need. A strong attachment to the young mother's mother is a very important factor in the decision to shift residences, but available space and food also weigh heavily. In large families it is often difficult to feed all of the children. When this is the case, at least one child, and sometimes several, will move to their grandmother's house as Bruce Orange did when he moved into Martha's house. Martha and Bruce each said that they felt like mother and son.

Some children or young adults went to live with a grandmother because they knew that the grandmother would be more tolerant than their own parents. A grandmother's love in some families is equal to or stronger than the mother's love. As long as there is an older woman still living with the family, the youngest members of the family often remain in some sort of dependent relationship with her. It is not at all unusual to find men and women forty and forty-five years old who still depend heavily upon an older woman in the family not only for help with decisions, but for money as well.

The oldest woman in the Hammon Cheyenne society, who is a grandmother and often a great-grandmother, will almost always be in a position of authority in her extended family. The degree of authority, will vary a great deal depending on her physical state, personality, and economic resources. One can detect a decline in the grandmother's authority if there is a decline in her physical state, in which case she is treated with guarded respect and kindness.

The Cheyenne grandmother is an important conservative voice of reason in the family and serves as the Navajo grandmother (Shepardson 1970:91–92) to keep alive the old tribal ways. She is the one who is constantly putting pressure on the rest of the family to maintain the traditional way of doing things and to adhere to past Indian values. Frequently, family members disagree with her views or may regard them with tender amusement, but they generally respect her, and they continue to consult her on important family matters.

One custom that indicates a growing importance of the grandmother in the Cheyenne family is the naming of children. It has always been a traditional custom for the grandfather to name a new grandchild. The child was usually named after a relative who had performed some heroic deed or who had a beautiful or respected name. For example, Anna Hawk was named after her grandmother, First Killer. The grandmother had been named after a Cheyenne who, many years ago, had been the first person to kill an enemy in a raid. Many of the older Cheyenne have Indian names that were given by their grandfathers. Today, the parents usually give the English name, but in Hammon the grandmother increasingly gives the Indian name to the child rather than the grandfather.

Cheyenne grandmothers today live in a rapidly changing world. In spite of their geographical and social isolation, the majority of them understand the importance of their grandchildren getting a good education so that they do not have to live trapped below the poverty line all of their lives.

Chapter Fifteen

"AN INDIAN CARES FOR EVERYBODY"

We Cheyennes help each other out. We share our things. That's the Indian way. An Indian cares for everybody. If he sees another Cheyenne who needs help, then he gives it to him. He doesn't want to be paid back. That's not the Indian way, bein' selfish and greedy, always wantin' to be paid back. If a man needs help, how can he pay back? The Indian is different than the whites. We say, "We know your ways. We talk your language, but you don't talk our language or know the Cheyenne ways."

--Martha Fingernail

The kinship ethic dictates that one must help any needy relative. Since the bonds of kinship extend so far in the community, one is obligated to help almost everyone else. The needs of families are often so great compared to their available resources that it is impossible for them ever to have enough money for the two most important expenses: utilities and food. Often families have to make a choice between the two.

The importance of sharing is especially acute in a society always coping with scarcity. As Evans-Pritchard (1940: 85) said of the Nuer in Africa: "This habit of share and share alike is easily understandable in a community where everyone is likely to find himself in difficulties from time to time, for it is scarcity and not sufficiency that makes people generous since everybody is thereby ensured against hunger. He who is in need today receives help from him who may be in need tomorrow."

Like the Yaqui located in northern Mexico and in communities and barrios near Tucson, Arizona, the assumption that relatives should share resources, tender aid, extend hospitality, and provide services is deeply ingrained in the Cheyenne code of ethics. The obligations are so diffuse that everything offered to or requested by relatives may be construed as forming part of these obligations (Kelley 1978: 51).

A pause in the powwow parade for Max Malone who is in a wheelchair. His wife, Jan, is standing on his left. On the far left can be seen two of the nine drummers. Author's Photo. 2004.

In some communities this generosity is disappearing. Benally (1999: 48–49) quotes a Navajo grandmother's lament for the disappearance of the reciprocity precept in her community: "During our younger days, people helped one another a lot. It was just a general practice they had. In the old days, even if a stranger came to the house, we would feed them and give them coffee. People aren't like that anymore. I think that it' s the trend. All over it's like that. Families would rather be responsible for their own immediate family these days, not for their relatives."

Anna Hawk, looking at her broken sewing machine, lamented: "That woman wanted my sewing machine and I let her have it. I needed it, but I let her have it anyway. And then she broke it so I don't know what I'm gonna' do. But I knew I had to help because someday I may need help too. I'm gettin' old and things might really get bad. I'll need somebody to help me out then."

Cheyenne women, especially older ones, constantly put pressure on all their neighbors to share, thereby perpetuating Indian values. Because theirs is a society of scarcity, it is very important that no family be allowed to subscribe to what they perceive as white values of individualism, achievement, and getting ahead, which puts an emphasis on the individual accumulation rather than a sharing of material goods.

The majority of transactions involving the transfer of goods, food, or money are putatively altruistic which is a characteristic in societies that have close kinship ties. Missing is even a vagueness of an obligation to reciprocate, and it does not stop the flow of goods from a giver to a recipient whether from need or desire.

The most common manifestation of Indian generosity without expecting a return is the Indian powwow that is a gathering of Indians who sing and dance and give goods and money to each other in the giveaway. Of the two most common forms of powwows, one is given at the tribal level by an individual or family to honor someone for an achievement. The other form is the annual summer powwow, a large, intertribal affair, sponsored by a joint tribal committee. Whether large or small, the powwow among the Cheyenne is always part of the Sun Dance or the Arrow Ceremony when they take place.

During the nomadic and reservation periods, men acquired status and prestige by distributing captured horses and giving them to the aged, the poor, and relatives. When the Cheyenne were confined to the reservation, the horse herds began to increase due to superior grazing land on the reservation. Status and prestige for men on the reservation were in part derived from a non-formalized giveaway system and the main item distributed was the horse. During the late 1910s and early 1920s, the Bureau of Indian Affairs reduced the number of horses in order to raise more cattle. When the horse population was decreased, the "table" began to replace the horse as a prime giveaway item. Given away as a unit, the table's value was supposed to be equal to that of a horse. Today's typical table consists of enamel pots and pans, dishes, food, a quilt or shawl, and yard goods—all women's items. Weist (1973) points out that then it is the women, not the men, who are acquiring prestige for their families. One of the most prestigious gifts today is the Pendleton blanket. Many of these blankets are taken home, put in a closet, and given away at the next giveaway. What is amazing is that Cheyennes, as impoverished as they are, always manage to have goods that they give away at the powwows.

In January 2005, Max Malone, the former pastor of the Indian Baptist Church in Hammon, announced that he had just been diagnosed with rapidly progressing leukemia. He was only fifty-eight, but his prognosis was grim. He was given a choice—to be treated with both chemotherapy and/or radiation and perhaps prolong his life by one month or an unknown number of months, or he could refuse the treatments and let the cancer take its course. He turned down the radiation and chemotherapy treatments, both of which have a number of side effects, and resigned his position with the Southern Baptist American Indian ministries. The news spread quickly through the Cheyenne and Arapaho communities, and a Saturday night dance was planned to honor his retirement—a powwow with dinner, gift-giving, participant and performance dancing, singing, and a chance to see old friends and neighbors who no longer lived close by.

The response was overwhelming. Approximately three hundred Cheyenne and Arapaho attended the gathering that started about two in the afternoon. It was held in the gymnasium of the Yukon High School located in a suburb of Oklahoma City. The flood of tributes was a total surprise to Max and his family, but the Cheyenne were showing their appreciation and love in the most special way they could, with a powwow. It was an expression of gratitude for the many hours he had spent ministering to their needs.

The celebration began with an emcee announcing the purpose of the gathering and introducing the honoree and his family who were sitting and standing in front of the stage. Max was in a wheelchair. His wife and most of their ten children (seven of whom had been adopted) with their spouses and children were standing beside him. Then he and his family moved to the opposite end of the gymnasium and followed the color guard entry down the length of the gym. In the middle of the floor, six drummers sat in a small circle around the large drum providing a steady drumbeat. It caught on quickly and prompted people to form a large circle around the smaller circle, holding hands and dancing (stepping sideways) to the beat of the drummers. The singers chimed in and the dancers who were going to perform later joined the circle. Each person who participated wore a piece of Indian clothing, a blanket or shawl, moccasins, a decorative hair piece, or a headdress, and there were a few full-length, richly decorated beaded dresses. The evening included a hearty meal for everyone attending, tributes made, and a giveaway of money and gifts in between songs and dances to the beat of the drums.

Giving these items with no explicit hope of return, especially to someone who would be totally unable to make a return, is true generosity. Generalized reciprocity in the example of the powwow is putatively altruistic, with nothing material expected in return. The most important benefit to the giver is prestige.

Anna Hawk explained that she had difficulty turning down a request for money even if she needed the money herself. Looking at a pair of partially finished beaded moccasins, she lamented, "This woman brought these to me and said, 'I need money to feed my children for the rest of the month. I want to sell these moccasins to you.' But I didn't want 'em. I told her I would take 'em for a while, and I gave her $10. I don't know why she never has any money because her family gets four checks a month. I needed the money, but someday I'll need help from somebody, too. I feel I have to help if I can."

If one Cheyenne has something that another Cheyenne likes, then the item is likely to change hands. Anna Hawk explained: "When someone comes up to me and says, 'That's a pretty purse,' I give it to them. I might say, 'That's a pretty dress,' and then they would give me their dress. Material things don't mean nothin'. When you die they're all gone. It don't matter."

Some transactions are not altruistic because they stipulate returns of commensurate worth or utility within a finite and narrow period. They are only negotiated in situations when it is reasonable to expect a return. In the majority of transactions, one cannot expect a return because many individuals never have any kind of economic fortune befall them to obtain something to exchange.

The daily intimacy created by the constant interacting among kin ensures that any change in a family's resources becomes news. Nothing can be kept a secret. Everyone knows who is working, when welfare checks arrive, and when additional resources are available. If an individual sells a piece of land or several pairs of moccasins for a good price or gets a temporary job hauling hay, this information is immediately circulated.

The ethic of sharing on such a large scale is part of the communal philosophy, and it allows the community to survive. The degree of impoverishment in the Indian community is so great that everyone who has a resource must share. Women, because of their greater resources, assume the primary responsibility for seeing that no one has to starve. Certainly, men help all they can, but if they are unemployed, their resources are limited. Out of necessity, they must turn to women for help.

Chapter Sixteen

PILLARS OF STRENGTH

This land for centuries belonged to everyone to use and enjoy but no one to own, a philosophy that translated into freedom for the indigenous peoples of America. They could roam and inhabit wherever they chose. Their philosophy conflicted drastically with the European position that land was meant to be owned or possessed as private property. Beginning in the fifteenth century as the British, Spanish, Portuguese, Dutch, and French fanned out across the continent, claiming ownership wherever they placed their stakes, an autonomous Cheyenne population was gradually losing the right to physically and spiritually nurture themselves at will from the land. The result? For many of the Europeans and their heirs, early land occupation of this yet undiscovered area would provide a future of prosperity. For others, the indigenous Hammon Cheyenne Indians and their heirs, it was a loss of their livelihood.

Today their land can be likened to a small, desolate impoverished island surrounded by a sea of prosperity, oil. The European aliens, who became Americans, soon owned most of the acreage and mineral rights to the oil, and the indigenous people, except for a few, lost their land by legal and fraudulent means. The future looks brighter as education becomes more valued, and discrimination fades. Solutions to the crippling poverty of Indians can gradually be solved for those who understand the importance of learning a marketable skill. Educational opportunities are boundless for those who are determined to finish their education. Many of the best universities, large and small, across the country have generous scholarships for anyone with a minimum of one-quarter Indian blood quantum.

The success of the Indian within the Anglo-Saxon culture in this country would be very precarious without the existence of extended family ties. The tenacity with which the Indian holds to the family bond under the most adverse circumstances provides a remarkable strength of which few cultures can boast.

Whites, who for the most part function in nuclear families and put a high value on material possessions, often have difficulty understanding the selflessness which Indians exhibit even to their most distant kin. A Cheyenne woman who is committed to her kin is preserving the kin's livelihood and well being in an unfriendly white world. The moral support that comes from strong bonds between female relatives provides a crucially cohesive element in Cheyenne family life. Bonds between men are also quite viable and operate in certain circumstances, most notably in the Arrow Ceremony that is exclusively for men, but those bonds do not provide the persevering support that bonds between women do. Cheyenne female bonds are of more importance because they accomplish two functions in Cheyenne society that are critical for survival. First, by being strongly oriented to children, they inculcate a sense of the importance of preserving the family. Second, by fostering economic cooperation, they provide a critical resource for day-to-day economic survival.

Gaining an overall understanding of the concept of grandmother-focused first requires a recognition of its complex factors that vary a great deal so that the degree of matrifocality may not be as intense in one group of kindred as in another. But the fact that groups of female kin can operate successfully in emergency situations, even if they are relatively inactive during other times, is significant. There is always the tacit knowledge that female kin can be counted on.

The loss of the male financial contribution to the family, which is the cumulative result of a century of prejudice, discrimination, and misguided government policies, has been critical for contemporary Cheyenne families. Men are highly valued, but no one in the Cheyenne community has the capability to provide them with jobs. Government programs such as CETA provide temporary economic relief, but any long-term benefit has not materialized. The year 2002 surge in oil-field activity in Roger Mills County and surrounding counties of Beckham, Washita, and Custer bodes well for Cheyenne employment opportunities, if oil production can be sustained, But, the loss of the male family role has had significant social repercussions for the family.

While it is true that females have more access to employment and welfare than males, economics is only part of the explanation. For example, a female who is employed, will undoubtedly call on her mother or another female relative to care for her children. But when looking at the child shifting pattern, we find that employment of the mother is only one of many reasons causing the grandmother to assume care of a child. More frequently, circumstances do not necessitate physical separation of mother and child--divorce, remarriage, insufficient economic resources, or simply an unwillingness to assume full care of a child, are more responsible for fosterage or shifting of children than just the employment of the mother. In fact, the readiness with which females shift children communicates a strong dependency relationship of young mothers on female family members who dutifully assume full responsibility for the care of the child or share that responsibility with other female family members. The young mothers may feel inadequate, or they may think that grandmother is the best person to watch over their babies. This relationship is nurtured over the years to the extent that it is quite common to find sons and/or daughters who are unable or unwilling to break out of this relationship, thus remaining dependent upon mother or grandmother even as late as age forty and beyond.

The hypothesis that the grandmother is structurally central to the family, that she has some degree of control over the kin unit's economic resources and is critically involved in kin-related decision-making processes, is substantiated in this study by a combination of family histories, household composition, sex ratio, and documentation of economic resources for women. These are the tangible characteristics of a grandmother oriented family. Yet there is no question that her role is highly important because it is so critical to survival. It is difficult, however, to argue that young Cheyenne girls are consciously socialized

181

to ultimately assume a strong decisive central kin role. In general, they are not. Older women do not insist that their daughters accept increasing responsibility in preparation for the assumption of this role, and few daughters actually seek responsibility, but many learn by example.

In some families, male and female siblings are competitive and jealous of each other to the extent that one may not permit another to ascend to a position of authority. But after a few years in most families this role can be filled by someone from the succeeding generation. Three important factors allow this to happen almost automatically: timing, health, and sex ratio.

When a grandmother who invariably is a widow (as the sex ratio indicates) vacates a position of authority either through physical incapacitation or death, her children, whether there are five, eight, or ten, will not all be in equal contention for her role. By the time her sons and daughters reach forty plus, there is a statistical probability that poor health and/or alcoholism will have taken a significant toll among them so that only one or two are physically able to assume this role. If no one in the second generation is able to ascend to this position, a granddaughter may do so. Competition in the granddaughter's generation is almost nonexistent because their attentions are directed elsewhere.

R. T. Smith (1993:139–142) notes that "the type of domestic unit found in any particular case is a result of the balance struck between the obligations of marriage and parenthood on the one hand and those due to matrilineal kin on the other."

The capacity to reach out to all kin through matrifocality in times of crises has enabled the Cheyenne family to remain strong. Their resourcefulness and perpetuation of Indian values are their ultimate defenses to the hostile culture of the white man. In economics and subsistence, matrifocality serves as an adaptive strategy that copes well with the ever present conditions of abject poverty. In a continual process of cooperative exchanges and giving, Cheyenne women maintain the viability of family and cultural traditions in the community. They are true pillars of strength.

References Cited

I. Archival Materials

A. Concho, Oklahoma

Cheyenne and Arapaho Report. 1973.

Johnson O'Malley files. 1992, 1999, 2006.

B. Bethel, Kansas

Hart, Lawrence. 2005. Cheyenne Legacy at the Washita River. Historical Committee & Archives of the Mennonite Church.

C. Hammon, Oklahoma

Hammon Cheyenne Family and Tribal Record Book: 1832–1974.

Hammon Indian Baptist Church records. The History of the Hammon Indian Mission. 1974.

D. Oklahoma City, Oklahoma.

Oklahoma Historical Society. Washita Oral History Project. 1999.

Oklahoma Medical Research Foundation. A Gift from Red Moon: Remembering a Frontier Physician. *Findings*. Fall 2004.

E. Red Rock, Oklahoma Civil Rights Hearing. Oklahoma Human Rights Commission, April 26, 1977.

II. Government Documents

U.S. Congress. Report of the Commissioner of Indian Affairs, 1892–1923.

U.S. Department of Agriculture. Economic Research Service, 2004.

U.S. Department of Commerce. Bureau of Census. *Characteristics of the Population*, 2004.

U.S. Department of Commerce. *Census of Agriculture*. Part 36, Section 2. 1969.

U.S. Department of Health, Education and Welfare, Public Health Service. *Indian Health Trends and Services*, 1970, 2000–2004.

Oklahoma State Department of Health. *Oklahoma Vital Record Statistics: Selected Demographic Profile* by County. 1970, 2000–2004.

III. Newspapers

Elk City, Oklahoma. *Elk City Daily News.*

Hammon, Oklahoma. *Hammon Advocate.*

Hammon, Oklahoma. *Hammon News.*

Oklahoma City, Oklahoma. *The Daily Oklahoman.*

Oklahoma City, Oklahoma. *Oklahoma Journal*

Watonga, Oklahoma. *Watonga Republican*

IV. Electronic Sources

http://indianz.com/News/archive/000355.asp (accessed February 7, 2006).

V. Books and Articles.

Benally, Karen Ritts. 1999. Thinking Good: The Teachings of Navajo Grandmothers. *American Indian Grandmothers: Traditions and Transitions*. M. Schweitzer, ed. Albuquerque: University of New Mexico Press.

Berthrong, Donald J. 1963. *The Southern Cheyennes*. Norman: University of Oklahoma Press.

_____.1972. Federal Indian Policy and the Southern Cheyennes and Arapahos 1887–1907. *The Western American Indian*. Richard Ellis, ed. Lincoln: University of Nebraska Press.

_____.1976. *The Cheyenne and Arapaho Ordeal: Reservation and Agency Life in the Indian Territory, 1875–1907*. Norman: University of Oklahoma Press.

Bittle, William E. 1954. The Peyote Ritual of the Kiowa Apache. *Oklahoma Anthropological Society*. Bulletin 2: 69–78.

Bott, Elizabeth. 1957. *Family and Social Network*. London: Tavistock Publications Ltd.

Brill, Charles J. 2001. *Custer, Black Kettle, and the Fight on the Washita*. Norman: University of Oklahoma Press. (Orig. pub. 1938).

Chinas, Beverly. 2002. *The Isthmus Zapotecs: A Matrifocal Culture of Mexico*. 2nd ed. (Orig. pub. 1973) Belmont, California: Wadsworth/Thompson Learning.

Eggan, Fred. 1955. The Cheyenne and Arapaho Kinship System. *Social Anthropology of North American Tribes*, 2nd ed. Fred Eggan, ed. Chicago: University of Chicago Press. (Orig. pub. 1937).

Evans-Pritchard, E.E. 1955. *The Nuer*. Oxford: Clarendon Press.

Fowler, Loretta. 2002. *Tribal Sovereignty and the Historical Imagination: Cheyenne Arapaho Politics.* Lincoln: University of Nebraska Press.

Geertz, Hildred. 1961. *The Javanese Family: A Study of Kinship and Socialization.* New York: Free Press of Glencoe, Inc.

Gonzales, Nancy. 1969. *Black Carib Household: A Study in Migration and Modernization.* Seattle: University of Washington Press.

Goody, Esther. 1968. *Fostering in Gonja Deprivation or Advantage?* ASA Monograph 6. London: Tavistock Publications.

_____.1973. *Contexts of Kinship: An Essay in the Family Sociology of the Gonja of Northern Ghana.* Cambridge: University Press.

Goody, Jack. 1969. Adoption in Cross-Cultural Perspective. *Comparative Studies in Society and History.* 11: 55–78.

Grinnell, George B. 1923. *The Cheyenne Indians: Their History and Ways of Life.* 2 vols. Lincoln: University of Nebraska Press.

Hale, Duane K. 1992. Uncle Sam's Warriors: American Indians in World War II. *Chronicles of Oklahoma.* 69 (4): 408–429.

Hedlund, Ann Lane. 1999. Give and Take: Navajo Grandmothers and the Role of Craftswomen. *American Indian Grandmothers,* M. Schweitzer, *ed.* Albuquerque: University of New Mexico Press.

Hinz-Penner, Raylene. 1966. Writing a Life. *Mennonite Life*(3) September.

_____.2007. *Searching for Sacred Ground: The Journey of Chief Lawrence Hart, Mennonite.* Telford, Pennsylvania: Cascadia.

Hodge, Patt. 1966. The History of Hammon and the Red Moon School. *The Chronicles of Oklahoma.* 44 (2): 130–139.

Hoebel, E. Adamson. 1960. *The Cheyennes: Indians of the Great Plains.* New York: Holt, Rinehart and Winston.

Hoig, Stan. 1992. *People of the Sacred Arrows: The Southern Cheyennes Today.* Norman: University of Oklahoma Press.

Hudson, Charles. 1976. *The Southeastern Indians.* Knoxville: University of Tennessee Press.

Ireson-Doolittle, C. and G. Moreno-Black. 2004. *The Lao: Gender, Power, and Livelihood.* Boulder: Westview Press.

Jablow, Joseph. 1951. *The Cheyenne in Plains Indian Trade Relations 1795–1840.* American Ethnological Society, Monograph No. 19.

Kelley, Jane Holden. 1978. *Yaqui Women: Contemporary Life Histories.* Lincoln: University of Nebraska Press.

Linscheid, Ruth. 1973. *Red Moon.* Newton, Kansas: United Printing.

Llewellyn, E.N. and E.A. Hoebel. 1941. *The Cheyenne Way: Conflict and Case Law in Primitive Jurisprudence.* Norman: University of Oklahoma Press.

Meadows, William C. 1999. *Kiowa, Apache, and Comanche Military Societies.* Austin: University of Texas Press.

Mooney, James. 1907. *The Cheyenne Indians.* Memoir 1, Washington, DC: American Anthropological Association.

Moore, John H. 1974. Cheyenne Political History, 1820–1894. *Ethnohistory* 21(4): 329–359.

_____.1987. *The Cheyenne Nation.* Lincoln: University of Nebraska Press.

_____.1996. *The Cheyenne.* Oxford, UK: Blackwell Publishers.

Parker, Kay. 1986. American Indian Women and Religion on the Southern Plains. *Women and Religion in America, 1900 to 1968. Vol.3.* Rosemary Reuther and Rosemary Keller, eds. San Francisco: Harper & Row.

Peery, Dan W. The Indians' Friend, John H. Seger. *Chronicles of Oklahoma.* 11 (2): 845–868.

Petersen, Karen Daniels. 1971. *Plains Indian Art from Fort Marion.* Norman: University of Oklahoma Press.

Petter, Rodolphe. 1936. *Reminiscences of Past Years in Mission Service Among the Cheyenne.* Private Printing.

Powell, Peter J. 1969. *Sweet Medicine: The Continuing Role of the Sacred Arrows, the Sun Dance and the Sacred Buffalo Hat.* 2 vol. Norman: University of Oklahoma Press.

Schweinfurth, Kay P. 2002. *Prayer on Top of the Earth: The Spiritual Universe of the Plains Apaches.* Boulder: University Press of Colorado.

Schweitzer, Marjorie. 1999. Introduction. *American Indian Grandmothers: Traditions and Transitions.* Marjorie Schweitzer, ed. Albuquerque: University of New Mexico Press.

Segalen, Martime. 1996. *Historical Anthropology of the Family.* New York: Cambridge Press. (Orig. pub. 1986).

Shepardson, M. and B. Hammond. 1970. *The Navajo Mountain Community.* Berkeley: University of California Press.

Smith, Raymond T. 1956. *The Negro Family in British Guiana: Family Structure and Social Status in the Villages.* London: Routledge.

_____.1973. The Matrifocal Family. *The Character of Kinship.* Jack Goody, ed. 121–144. Cambridge: Cambridge University Press.

_____.1996. The *Matrifocal Family: Power, Pluralism, and Politics*. London: Routledge.

Stack, Carol B. 1975. *All Our Kin: Strategies for Survival in a Black Community*. New York: Harper and Row.

Stephan, Lynn. 2005. *Zapotec Women: Gender, Class, and Ethnicity in Globalized Oaxaca*. 2nd Rev & Up. Raleigh: Duke University Press.

Stewart, Omer C. 1987. *Peyote Religion: A History*. Norman: University of Oklahoma Press.

Tanner, Nancy. 1974. Matrifocality in Indonesia and Africa and Among Black Americans. Michelle Rosaldo and Louise Lamphere, eds. *Woman, Culture, and Society*. Stanford: Stanford University Press.

Weist, Kathryn. 1973. Giving Away: The Ceremonial Distribution of Goods Among Northern Cheyenne of Southeastern Montana. *Plains Anthropologist*. (18): 97–103.

Will, George. 1913. The Cheyenne Indians in North Dakota. *Proceedings of the Mississippi Valley Historical Association for the Year 1913–1914*. (7). Cedar Rapids.

Wong, Kate. 2006. The Morning of the Modern Mind. *Scientific A0merican*. 16: 2.

Index

Y

Z

www.ingramcontent.com/pod-product-compliance
Lightning Source LLC
Chambersburg PA
CBHW061353280526
45784CB00001B/240